What Was Lost

Also by Herbert Morris

Peru

Dream Palace

The Little Voices of the Pears

What Was Lost

Herbert Morris

COUNTERPOINT

WASHINGTON, D.C.

"To Baden," "The Hall, the Hall Grown Cold," and "Jack Waiting"
first appeared in *Boulevard*.
"House of Words" and "Sophia and Marcello on a Bench" first
appeared in *Denver Quarterly*.
"On the Plight of Us in the Caravaggio" and "Joyce on the French
Coast Waiting for the Dark" first appeared in *The Kenyon Review*.
"Opera" and "Ultimate Poem" first appeared in *The New Criterion*.
"Duesenberg, 1929" first appeared in *Poetry*.
"Approaching a City" first appeared in *The Quarterly*.
"One Hundred Versions of the Peaceable Kingdom," "Certain
Mysteries Flowing from the Gown," and "Now the Fitzgerald
Brothers Growing Older" first appeared in *Salmagundi*.
"History, Weather, Loss, the Children, Georgia" first appeared in
The Yale Review.

Library of Congress Cataloging-in-Publication Data
Morris, Herbert
What was lost / Herbert Morris.
p. cm.
ISBN 1-58243-064-0 (alk. paper)
I. Title.
PS3563.O87434 W48 2000
811'.54—dc21   99-087231

Book design by David Bullen

Printed in the United States of America on acid-free paper that
meets the American National Standards Institute z39-48 Standard

Counterpoint
P. O. Box 65793
Washington, DC 20035-5793

Counterpoint is a member of the Perseus Books Group.

For the singer in "Opera"

it is cold in the car, yet we keep warm

Contents

What Was Lost

House of Words

Henry James, Rye, 1906

I had the most disturbing dream this morning.
Alvin Langdon Coburn had come to call
yesterday, in the afternoon, at four,
accompanied by proof plates of the portrait
for which, some time past, he proposed I sit
and for which, a fortnight ago, I sat.
The good man stayed to tea, at my behest;
we spoke of the weather, light, the variables
of the English countryscape—only now
is he coming to know it—, its foul moods,
its fair ones, tones, half-tones, tones undeciphered,
his aspirations, which, given his youth,
seem quite remarkable for breadth, for scope,
the vision—he has that in full—entailed,
what he proposes for himself, those projects
entertained, an informal "master plan,"
as it were, no less urgent, visionary,
wanting nothing whatever of ambition,
for the informality of its nature,
should he follow his instincts, which exceed,
in conception, daring, sympathy, beauty,
vastly exceed, all that has come before this,
that to which he has put his mind, his eye,
when he might, in his words, "transcend oneself,"
though he is just beginning (there is time,
I reassured him, there is time on your side);
spoke of the vagaries of photographic
portraiture, as he sees them, and to which
the gentleman has not, to hear him tell it,

accustomed himself, wholly made his peace with,
followed by the man's pained, detailed recital
(admirably restrained, almost reluctant),
albeit cogent, moving, of dilemmas
in willing mere mechanical devices,
lens, timer, shutter, dimmest "apparatus"
(quiescent, mindless until now, awaiting
someone—oneself—to rouse them into life),
to reproduce, as best they can, that vision
one possesses as much as is possessed by—
one's version of the world, one thinks to call it—,
the problem, too, with words, if I may say so,
dilemmas, in all truth, with which I am not,
nor ever have been, a fine point made finer,
wholly—irredeemably—unfamiliar.

More of Mr. Coburn's photograph later.
I saw the man out to the gate, walked with him
the full length of the path, where the road meets it—
he had traveled from London, hesitant,
fearful, craving, one felt, one's good opinion,
should I not wholly fail to read the scene right,
regarding one's appraisal of his efforts:
wanting it, sorely wanting it, the need,
should one dare peer into its face, quite naked
(yes, a keen likeness, quite fine, I assured him;
how the man beamed, how the praise energized,
suffused, transformed, made vivid his demeanor,
this young man, all the years, or all the choices,
opening to the future, this youth, trim,
handsome, stylish, even, in the extreme).
We walked, as I have written, to the road,
where a carriage, soon due, would take him back
to that small, cramped studio, to the life,
from which he had set out to make his way
that morning, early, by degrees, to Rye—

a pilgrimage touchingly deferential,
surely, given his projects, his work habits,
and his penchant for making that dim workshop,
cluttered with tools, equipment, apparatus,
the center of his life, if not his life.
He took my hand, smiled, thanked me, then stood silent;
nonplused, even embarrassed (gratitude
unmerited: one's deep discomfiture
seems, on the face of it, inevitable,
a sinking, as it were, to the occasion;
was it not I who should have grasped his hand,
should have extended himself as we stood there,
eerily silhouetted in that twilight
gathering about us, crowding our shoulders,
I who should have made overtures, have given
some merest indication, made some gesture,
not yet a word, not yet that, a mere gesture,
to convey to him deference, respect,
gratitude — a young man coming such distance,
such great distance; I the one to have smiled,
have expressed thanks, however poorly, dimly,
in however shy or partial the fashion,
I the one to have stood before him silent,
Henry James the transformed one, the "transcendent"?),
I turned, turned to leave, this small house, Lamb House,
my name on the deed in a steel-clad vault
in the lower depths of the Bank of England,
this plot, this patch, this acre, this failed garden,
seeming all at once to offer escape
at the end of the path, tall grass on all sides,
uncut, untamed, untended — surface calm,
a seething just beneath it —, from confusion,
illness-at-ease, unsettledness, disruption,
from — one fails, quite fails, to know what to call it —
intimations of extreme dislocation
(escape, too, more profoundly, from those things

whose name eludes one for the moment, forces
one gropes for reasons not to have to name),
felt an exhaustion, opening the door,
out of all proportion to the day's labor,
which, at best, had been meager, negligible
(Coburn's visit had taken place precisely
at that hour, to one's regret, the author
would, in fact, be found at his writing table,
should the day have progressed uninterrupted,
embarking, hoping shortly to embark,
on his work for the afternoon, his task;
until such time as the man took his leave,
clutching those proof plates to himself as fiercely
as his hope to win the subject's approval—
yes, a keen likeness, quite fine, I assured him,
finding strengths in them rightfully another's,
blurring weaknesses much, too much, one's own—,
little had been transcribed on paper, nothing).

Determined not to nap nor yet succumb
to that fatigue which all but overwhelmed me,
a fatigue, oddly, for which explanation,
any and all, shall prove quite unavailing
(Coburn?, his call?, his gratitude?, his bearing?,
one's unresponsiveness, that seeming coldness
which wished him gone that, alone, one might work?),
I turned directly to the sheaf of notes
written the day before, descriptive matter,
exploratory passages (perhaps
a long story, just begun, just beginning,
anonymous, amorphous, weightless, shapeless,
struggling to free itself—one feels its movement,
its struggle—from the dimness, one's own dimness,
nothing more, nothing less, in which it lies,
still in flux, all too likely, at this stage,
to rise, rise from the page, flee, disappear,

should one say too much of it, and too soon)
linking aspects of landscape, season, setting,
details of background, to those personages
(W, A) on the verge, as it were,
of making entrances, their introductions,
débuts, as one now sees it, more a matter
of light, of weather, than of character,
only later that correspondence drawn,
glimpsed, later, after there shall have evolved
turns of plot in which motives lie embedded
deep in common ore, gold sifted, refined,
only later one's "décor" understood
as representing who these players are,
what, and before one's eyes, they have become,
what forces, then and now, may have impelled them,
the weight, the very texture, of their lives.

There followed what one brings oneself to call
a frenzy of activity, idea
yielding idea, image heaped on image,
illumination on illumination.
Darkness fell, yet one took scant notice of it,
looking up from one's notes, at that point, only
to discover one could no longer make out
pen on paper, words which one had transcribed;
it was then, only then, I turned the lamp up.
The writing bore specific gravity,
a density not normally forthcoming,
so it seemed, plot advancing character,
character, as one wished, advancing plot,
an interweaving of abstract and concrete,
symbol and object, fact, plain fact, and dream,
each nourishing on each, each, in turn, nourished;
if not yet passion, what might lead to passion,
if not yet fluency, at the least "flow."
One recalls, dimly, writing on and on,

through the night, flights of phrase, turns, double turns,
complications, intricacies, the half-tones
weighted with resonance beyond the whole tones,
embellishment past mere embellishment,
all splendidly entangled, layered, dense,
though the sense of it, time sense, quite escapes me,
writing as one had not written before,
driven to write, one might say; yes, that: driven.

When I awoke, head slumped across those notes
committed through the night, page upon page
(fingers, I would discover, flexed as though
still holding to the pen which once they held,
but for the fact the pen lay on the floor,
having dropped there when I fell off to sleep,
beside one's slipper; all the fingers held,
curled, vaguely contorted, was the queer shape,
gnarled, indrawn, cramped, clenched, broken, paralytic,
of the dream in which the hand, the right hand,
Henry James' right hand, had been raised, half raised,
to ward off the blow, the fierce blow, one knew,
knew as well as one could know anything,
would come down, come down soon, across one's head,
across, if but the truth were known, one's life),
light had broken, the little lamp beside me
still cast its pale, thin light across the room,
birdsong, though muffled, issued from the garden.
It was then, making my way to the window,
parting the drape, only then, I remembered
the dream, remembered, too, its grip, its terror,
one's abandonment to one's resignation
in the face of such closure, such entrapment—
utter disruption, utter desolation—,
the pulse-beat throbbing wildly at the temple,
the heart beginning to race faster, faster,
ready to burst forth from its cage, to cry

some cry of piercing strangeness, haunting, stricken,
dampness soaking the brow, staining the waistcoat,
fingers suffering nervous twitching spasms,
hands clammy, one's face ashen in the glass,
misshaped, disfigured, overnight grown old,
grown cold, grown all things alien, unfamiliar,
another's face, in truth, another's life.

It was the year I first settled in London
to which the dream gave transport, that first year,
when I had taken rooms in the West End,
the dream as clear as to time, weather, setting,
as the rest lies obscured, unsettled, murky,
much of one's daylight hours spent at a desk
overlooking the street, writing those tales,
"American" one called them then, which seem now
meager, anemic, thin in the extreme,
by evening, having been pressed to bear with me,
on departure, letters of introduction
to certain Mayfair houses to which entry
proved, would soon prove, one's passport to the world
(that wide, diverse world, London in the Eighties,
a society rich, complex, in flux,
almost exotic in its complications,
permutations, its possibilities,
the lengths to which, to one's reward, it might be
subject to the profoundest exploration,
fairly begging to be observed, recorded,
its levels shifting, moving upward, downward,
the movement dizzying to contemplate),
enjoying, at the time, a small, quite modest,
yet what one might call growing reputation—
those early tales, no doubt, in *The Atlantic*
(they had, it seemed, made the crossing from Boston,
frail vessels each, apparently intact,
stout little ships, despite what one feels now,

sailing forth unimpeded on strange waters,
brave in their ignorance of tides, of weather),
making one's way across that teeming city,
five or six evenings, frequently, each week,
at the height of the season, acquiescing
in the face of those pleas, often repeated,
prevailing upon one to make a fourth
("a small, intimate setting, I assure you,
as it is my conviction you most favor,
that, as you confessed at one such soirée here,
none of it lie beyond your scrutiny,
nothing escape you, be lost on you, nothing,
not their eyes, not their voices, their expressions,
their demeanor at table, nothing, nothing—
how insistent you were: oh, I remember
perfectly your passion—nothing lost, nothing")
at Princess Charlotte's table, or requesting
that one be in attendance at the dinner
the Viscountess Savoia would give marking
the first official state visit to London
of the Duchess de Alba's second daughter
("By your presence, should you so honor us,
shall we not, in our way, inform the Spanish,
in however understated a fashion,
English letters, as well, bear a tradition
quite as rich, quite as worthy, as the Latin,
that in our own tongue, too, there can be wrought,
by a master, something of grace, wit, beauty,
something durable, long surviving us?").

It was to dinner at Contessa Vitti's
one was, in the dream, slowly making progress,
the slowness as forbidding as the progress,
having, earlier, hailed a carriage, yielded
to the chap up front an address in Mayfair
to which, in a strong, firm voice, speaking plainly,

one expressed simply one's wish to be driven,
the chap's face, I might add here, for whatever
portent it may take on, never seen clearly
in the dark, twilight having fallen early,
inordinately early, so one thought,
a darkness even then one sensed an omen,
the first, rude inklings of some total strangeness,
vast in scope yet all the while undeciphered,
bound, presently, to descend, to engulf one,
alter one's life, one's clear conception of it.
It was through back streets wholly unfamiliar
the driver now saw fit to make his way,
seemingly certain of where he was headed,
streets, one knew, which would never lead to Mayfair
but to more distant parts, a London other
than the London one knew, another city,
wholly another province of the senses.
His body swaying this way, that, the carriage
lurching to one side, then the other, wheel struts
clattering rut by rut (cobbles chipped, broken,
half-broken, that clipped rhythm as we crossed them
equally broken, equally half-broken,
dizzying, lulling, dangerous, hypnotic),
slipping, sliding, tottering, giving way,
the reins glowing eerily in his hands,
flowing out from them with unearthly light,
dust everywhere, obscuring background, foreground,
horizon turned to sky, sky to horizon,
blinding the gelding tethered to the carriage,
matting the chestnut coat, snared in the mane,
beneath its flanks four legs a tawny blur,
clotting gear spokes, jamming cotter pins, rib shaft,
soiling the grime-streaked leather where one gasped,
head thrown back on the cushion, in exhaustion,
ill-at-ease, queasy, fearful from the start,
gasped for breath, vision, sight, waited for light,

dust flaying eyes, mouth, evening cloak, silk waistcoat,
freshly buffed shoes, cravat, the visible
half-seen, the half-seen visible, one heard,
one thought one heard, a voice, the coachman's voice,
looming from somewhere in the dark above one,
a voice low, rasping, not a coachman's voice
nor a human voice, unidentified,
unidentifiable, these its words:
"These, Sir, are the approaches we have come to:
just beyond lies the City of Regret."

The bridges, bridge by bridge, spanning the Thames,
resplendent arched across unquiet waters,
were lined with coaches, carriages, all driving
("driven" may be the word) in one direction.
Avenues took up where each bridge left off,
boulevards so teeming, so densely packed,
streets so rich with the human element,
there seemed little room, none, in fact, for traffic
of horses, carriages, those not on foot,
while those on foot, crowds filling alleys, byways,
jostled for every inch of walking space,
breathing space. What might be their destination;
what, in concerted fashion, could have drawn them?
From each business establishment, each storefront,
from the shops, residences, rooming houses,
people streamed, strolling, milling, congregating,
river merging with river, tide with tide,
borne on the currents sweeping this way, that,
side streets, cross streets, avenues, boulevards.
Mayfair, Mayfair, I cried; are we near Mayfair?,
astonished at the sound of one's own voice,
pitch, timbre, urgency, tone of command,
the insistence with which one pleaded "Mayfair,"
the desperation of the late, the placeless,
panic lacing the plea, woven throughout.

Contessa Vitti: you must know the house,
a corner, two ash trees, facing the square,
that statue of a horse stripped of its rider—
what can its name be?—, surely you must know it.
Here, I will show you; we cannot be far—
but to no avail: in the dark one's voice
carried briefly, barely, quite failed to carry,
or the driver, poor chap, not visible
all this while, failed to hear, or merely half-heard,
or was perched elsewhere, past the range of words.
La Contessa, in Mayfair, I repeated,
that house—we must be near; here, I will show you—
with a façade of pale blue terra cotta
inlay, that overhang of slate from which
gargoyles and saints peer as the guests pull up
(clicking stone tongues, it seems, exchanging gossip).
Surely you know it; has no one before this
asked to be taken there—Contessa Vitti?

From the darkness of outskirts where we drove,
"approaches" to "the City of Regret"
(drove no longer: were swept forward best states it),
buoyed by currents buffeting us on all sides,
we now entered a sector of the city
given wholly, it seemed, to one's amusement,
gratification in whatever guise,
brightly lit, lights of theatres, cabarets,
music halls, dance halls, all conceivable
entertainments, divertissements, distractions,
even those not yet quite to be conceived of.
Lights rose everywhere, near side, far side, background,
foreground, everywhere, rose, fell back, rose once more,
only to fall, only once more to rise,
illuminating those gathered beneath them—
corners of parks, squares, curbsides, alleys, walkways,
throngs passing back and forth, to and fro, dance hall

to music hall, theatre to cabaret,
some relentless procession under light,
under lights, ebb, then flow, coming, then going,
with as little purpose, so it appeared,
attached to coming as attached to going
(the thinness of one's life, the very thinness),
its purposelessness possibly its charm,
its power to attract, astound, refresh,
to subvert, in a fashion unexpected,
fraught with surprise, those long-held preconceptions
as to the place of pleasure in one's life,
the role of idleness, of aimlessness
(once to be free, once, of incessant striving,
the need to fashion beauty, the long struggle
for loveliness, perfection, in one's life).
I, who had always held himself apart,
had cause to hold himself apart, from crowds,
others en masse, I who had found himself
never less than reluctant to plunge in,
to brave the onslaught of that tide, that wave,
more than hesitant to immerse oneself
in currents likely to sweep one far out,
that turbulence which raged past one's control,
that chaos from which there seems no way back;
I, finder of refuge, maker of refuge,
in words, whose life, indeed, was spun of words,
spun and respun, spun once more, then respun,
a life which has itself become a refuge
(words, in a world bordered by blood, on one side,
by the tumult of passion on the other;
the thinness, yes, the thinness of one's life:
what has one built if not a house of words?;
what can one's life have been said to have come to?),
ill-at-ease in the presence of that mingling,
those lights, that clamor, that life of the streets,
yet has not once flinched from such confrontation,

not once, on behalf of those many figures
of one's invention, social creatures each,
however great the distance from the center
at which their author stood, preferred to stand;
I, who had been spared, who had spared himself,
the difficult, profound, day-to-day labor
of action, interaction, going, coming,
here, in the midst of random, far-flung streets
where, from the rear seat of a carriage making
small progress, none whatever, through that traffic
of gathered multitudes, dust, fever, clamor,
one peers from left to right, on all sides, witness
to the rise and fall of an unknown city,
foreign, tumultuous, named for Regret;
I, Henry James, living these many years
in a small house in Rye suiting precisely
the sum of needs, small in equal proportion,
a man past his middle years still admits to,
a man, it now appears, destined to live out
what time remains to him in the same small house,
his needs, few from the start, still few, grown fewer,
settled, established, wanting nothing further
from his life than it gives, than, in abundance,
it has until now generously given,
wanting, in fine, nothing to change the pattern,
no alteration to be introduced now,
to intrude on the rhythm of the days,
stem the flow—dare one call it grace?, or peace?—
of season unto season, year to year,
I, who never before this have known envy,
caught, all at once, in the grip of a fever
of such dimension, a seizure of envy
so telling, so pervasive, so relentless,
it pains one now even in the recounting—
envy of those spilling into those streets
with such abandon, heedlessness, such spirit

of adventure, setting forth filled with courage,
fearless before all, all, they might encounter,
strolling those avenues, those boulevards,
bathed by that light which, everywhere ascendant,
cast such unearthly glow across their faces,
in search of—what to call it if not pleasure?,
envy of those, as well, whose very lives
were spent for that, unflagging, unrelenting,
"devoted," one might say, to such pursuit,
the justice of the term at once apparent
yet, for that, no less striking, no less apt.

It came to me, then, head back on the leather
seat of the carriage, one's brow burning, damp,
yet a chill wind stirring within the coach,
overcome by foreboding, dread, fatigue,
on the threshold, it seemed, of revelations
damaging by nature, leaving destruction
in their wake, one's breath coming short now, rapid,
a spasmodic heaving, irregular,
a seizure, as it were, of apprehension,
a gasp, a gasping, how, in certain lights—
that light which everywhere rose in those lanes,
those feverish dream streets, terrible, rich
with omens, visions, infinitely textured—,
there are lives, one's own life not least among them,
which seem, which come to seem, utterly wasted,
lived by the wrong means for the wrong ends, lived
at the edge, at some safe edge, at those edges
far from the center where most lives are lived,
where one's store of passion lodges, resides,
heat, essential heat, core of what is human.
It came to me, the inadvertence of it
fortuitous in the extreme (some insights
enter through a rear door, guests unexpected,
uninvited, all at once at the gate,

standing forlorn—invite them in?, refuse them?—,
empty-handed, or through a door located
nowhere, nowhere, though we have searched, searched long,
nowhere sketched on a blueprint of the house,
the very house of words, that very shelter,
one has drawn about oneself through the years
against what?—weather?, fall of darkness?, fall
of whatever elects, and soon, to fall?,
in that province bereft of any marker
indicating where we now find ourselves
one evening, late, without forewarning, lacking
explanation, all hope of explanation,
more profoundly, where we have lost ourselves),
that the life one has lived has been a spared life,
the single life one could have lived, yet spared,
at some remove from that essential center
where others live, some distance (vast, one fears)
from where, in fact, one's own life should have been lived,
inserted itself, risked, plunged deep, plunged deeper,
had one's first thought not been to spare oneself;
that, of the choices one might well have made,
it was this, this, one chose: that one be spared,
this overriding, taking precedence,
as the dream, much to one's astonishment,
horror, dismay, made glaringly apparent,
that one never again be caused to suffer
what one might call the grand theme, that motif
underlying the life each of us lives—
what one has risked, has failed to risk, for passion
(and the losses endured in either case),
never again to have those pages opened,
that particular chapter closed, quite closed,
that volume, at last, at last, sealed fast, shuttered,
all the attendant anguish lodged within it,
an anguish (malady of dislocation,
sorrow unendurable and abiding

in equal proportion—what shall one call it?,
its name of little consequence) one suffered
more than one's proper share of, more, much more,
in one's earlier years, the cause of which,
the nature, as it were, of the affliction,
one need not bring oneself to speak of here,
if, in truth, one were able (one is not,
one has never been, able, that upheaval,
the specter of missed chances, indecisions,
warring factions within one—some sweet truce
longed-for but not forthcoming—utter chaos,
seeming to loom forever past one's reach,
beyond that border where articulation
lies to one side, hard silence to the other,
a past, that part of a too-painful past,
to which all links are severed—not forgotten,
never forgotten, no, merely interred).

Alvin Langdon Coburn's portrait, alas,
revealing, as it happens, in those aspects
in which one might least welcome revelation,
might least wish to unearth the so-called truth,
shows an elderly gentleman (the skill
at his command, this humble picture-taker,
portrait-maker, whatever power in it,
whatever force behind it, unavailing
before the fact: how to turn age to youth?;
how to compose oneself before the lens
that one appear what, in fine, one is not?),
a man preoccupied, distracted, burdened,
care-worn, time-worn, overcome with fatigue,
wearing the years, I fear, with little grace,
the face lined, shadowed, aged, one recognized
not at all as one's own, a stranger's face,
someone one neither knows nor seeks to know,
a man under some strain, making the effort—

futile, utterly futile, yet, in context,
verging, it could be claimed, on the heroic—,
without demonstrable success, to fathom
(even a moment's clarity sufficing,
a mere, stray fragment, some vague, random glimmer)
what the years were, how one's life has been spent,
for what, the thing to which one gave oneself
(search for the word in which it lies, pronounce it,
find some approximation, shape it, speak it,
however insufficient, partial, plain,
whatever its inadequacy, maître,
wordsmith, plotter, spinner of tales, grand master);
a man for whom, it appears, it is late,
for whom, from the start, it was always late,
someone for whom the dream one has narrated,
that dream from which one woke here hours before,
bears one's markings, indelibly, across it,
one's prints, binds one's life more tightly within it
than the embrace of anything before this.

This, this man in the dream, is who one is;
search no longer for an identity
long-ago garbled, blurred, long-ago woven
into the fabric of the myths one spun—
can it be said whether one plots the tales
or is, equally, plotted by them, maître?
(say who spins whom, then; say, too, what the years were;
name the thing for which one's life has been spent:
find the word for it, wordsmith, one word, one).
This, I tell you, is the man, I, no other,
someone who has devised a house of words,
no more, no less, in which to live, assembled
slowly, with great care, year by year, a structure
of which it seems one took scant notice (blindness:
for all one's vaunted "vision," utter blindness)
until it stood there, towering above one,

finished, each word in place, all but complete,
late, too late, for the yes, the no, one might cry,
the weight it bears, the volume, vast, immense,
more than one thought a mere house might displace,
the sum, in short, of the years, one's true life;
someone who has placed himself in the hands,
much to his regret, of a carriage driver
who has been given an address in Mayfair
(La Contessa: surely you know the house)
only, later, much later, to discover
the coachman, never seen, has, all the while,
had small intention, no, none, none whatever,
of consenting to fulfill your request
(simple as it may, on its surface, seem,
however civilly, my dear chap, stated),
having planned, mind you, from the start, to drive you
where he has determined that you be driven—
the approaches, from sheer perversity
glittering and obscene, both, at the same time,
to this fabled city named for Regret,
as he so perspicaciously has termed it—,
nor of acceding to your plea, repeated
several times, that, once more, he attempt
(let me show you, I know the way) to find it,
saints and gargoyles gossiping in the gables,
repeated out of fear he fails to hear you,
traffic bearing down on all sides now, people
spilling to the street, raucous, clamorous,
the human element in fullest flower,
glancing upward, as one does, out of instinct,
one's custom in the past, in the direction
of where one thinks the driver sits, of where,
in ordinary contexts, drivers sit
(the context, granted, hardly ordinary),
having nothing in response, voice, a sign,
bat of an eye, human assent, dissent,

hearing only breathing in the dark, breathing
difficult, slow, laborious, afflicted
(someone lined, shadowed, aged, burdened, fatigued),
only the noise the heart makes, night to night,
the beat faint, distant, tremulous, imperfect
(despite one's "gift," one's "vision," utter blindness:
the thinness, oh, the thinness, of one's life),
looming on the horizon, dimly glimpsed,
if at all glimpsed, a house, maître, a great house,
lit from within, welcoming in the dark,
the only house one knew or seemed at home in,
in the approaches dusk already fallen
(late, shrunken, blind, here, let me show the way),
not, it seems, the Contessa's, not the house
to which one wished, setting out, to be taken
(whatever the intention of the driver,
the dream, the fixed idea, for whatever
purpose he bears in mind for you, this coachman,
this guider of the horse, giver of names—
a city, mind you, rising from Regret—,
this interloper, reins slack in his hands,
flowing with a perverse, uncommon light),
but a house, nonetheless, a destination,
a house rising, imagine, word by word,
from words, one's words (find the word for it, wordsman;
say, if you can, what the years were, one's life).

One Hundred Versions of
the Peaceable Kingdom

Edward Hicks painted the Peaceable Kingdom
over one hundred times.

Each one, no doubt, more perfect than the last,
should perfection consist of balances
harmonious not for the sake of eye,
eye alone, but that mind, mind, too, be pleased,

appeased, assuaged, comforted, calmed, cajoled,
the scene in its depiction shapely, rounded,
or, for the moment, drawn so, Edward, made so.
(What more is there to do, then, but console?)

Should disruption, entering through a gate
left unattended, unsecured, its presence
jarring, however guileless, here among us,
wholly, one might add, unpremeditated,

insinuate itself, intrude, subvert
the text, the music, all one can do, Edward,
is attempt to reach beyond dissonance,
turn back, begin, begin again, revise.

One understood, perhaps from the beginning,
how long it took, might take, to get it right
(ambition such as this consumes one's life),
to fix it for all time beneath this shade-tree,

the tracery of fronds, the sweep of branches,
the very breathing, rise and fall, of grass blades,
under a sky needing no alteration,
none whatever, that is, until the next time,

when the palpitations of each frail leaf,
clouds between two great larches, river upstream,
the comely beasts themselves, their eyes, their coats,
not least the way they nestle close, serene,

might be rendered with less equivocation,
greater fidelity to what one's dream,
one's vision, has determined be depicted.
What is to be offered but consolation?

Upstream, of course, the river broadening
to include everything one cannot say
about one's life, about the life imagined,
the current, in the distance, sweeping out

to where neither mind nor eye has yet traveled,
acres one calls, wishes to call, tomorrow
(terminology still uncertain, vague,
vocabularies still unformed, untested,

pale blues, pale greens, wash of obscure magentas,
shades assigned all things indeterminate,
colors best suited to the undefined,
reserved on maps for Regions Unexplored),

will be, must be, wholly another province,
lying past speculation, past regret,
its own turf, as it were, dabs of horizon
not wholly sky and yet not wholly water.

Let the colonists gather on embankments
situated as handsomely as this,
sloping gently to the river below,
prospects, on all sides, this richly endowed,

with the tribes of adjoining grassy shores,
tribes whose woods these are, have been, and shall be,
no matter what the charts, covenants, edicts,
true "ownership" established, "rights" laid claim to,

may, in their splendid arrogance, proclaim
("such lands as lie hereof, such deeds, such titles,
downstream, upstream, woods to bounteous woods,
deemed, in perpetuity, the Republic's"),

each in finery—waistcoats, gauntlets, tricorns,
greasepaint, chieftains' headdresses, capes of feathers—
befitting so auspicious an occasion,
a convocation this light-struck, this civil.

Let clouds billow as clouds have never billowed
between these larches breaking into flames.
Let the fox doze at the edge of a forest
nothing if not resplendently enchanted,

eyes closing, closed, triumphantly at ease
with itself, lush, green ground thatch, wood's sweet fragrance,
dim in this patch, this glade, where it will dream
a man arrives dispensing consolation

among them, paints them, in the process tames them,
a faint smile seeming to caress its jaw,
the tips of its ears glowing in the dark,
its fur blending with tree trunks. Let the snake,

spotted, dazzling garden variety,
drape its torso across the boughs above,
seductive in its languor, coils unfurled,
dally to view the beasts ensconced below,

the scene as someone, Edward, has arranged it,
this man turning on the embankment, trying,
trying again, at last to get it right,
one hundred versions, turning, then returning,

arranging, rearranging, the embankment
nothing if not the dream haunting the eye,
Edward, the light-struck, painter, dreamer, tamer.
What if not consolation shall one offer?

Let the lion, the lamb, the hare, the jackal,
the princely leopard, paws outstretched before it,
embodiment of grace, of trust abiding,
order in the universe, even creatures

one has failed, will fail, to identify,
those Edward has not yet taken to name,
lie becalmed, wholly without distraction,
oblivious to the details of weather,

to light, to how light breaks, to the concerns
of men, men meeting where the river bends,
tomorrow fanning out in all directions
upstream, a distance from here, past one's vision

(though, of course, Edward shows us little of that,
perhaps because he knows little himself),
an assembly convened beneath the larches,
courtliness in the air, even affection,

elements divers now on common ground
(dappled embankment, forest, river bend)
not fifty paces from where beasts recline,
animals named and those awaiting names,

fifty paces from which to view these men
with the supreme indifference of their species,
should they, even a moment, turn from Edward,
Edward, clothed in a charm which disconcerts,

perplexes, conquers, wholly mesmerizes,
unfix their gaze, undo their fascination,
erase, even a moment, from their minds
this image of a man standing before them,

easel, bristles, paint pots, gleaming blank canvas,
ready to do them justice, more than justice,
if he can, paint them slowly into myth,
instructing them to lie close, closer, nuzzle,

nestle in summer's dappled shade, attend
birdsong, regard leaf-stir, rustle of grasses
(what can one do here but console, console?;
is not the end of all earthly endeavor,

in such weather, such light, on this mere acre
allotted us, animals, to be kind?),
overcome, if perhaps not quite abandon,
their astonishment at how tender men are,

men can be, how fraught with uncommon feeling,
cease their bantering chatter, their beast noise,
the gutturals of lion, lamb, hare, jackal,
the syllables which issue from the snake,

so that this man, this solitary figure
standing half drenched with light, half plunged in shadow,
painter, consoler, tamer of the beasts,
the one others, they note, address as Edward,

can get them, get them right, once more attempt to,
do whatever men do intent on justice,
for a moment, a moment only, feel
what he must feel, if they can, see what he sees,

glimpse, as he glimpses, even from the corner
of a beast's eye, incandescence in woods,
unearthly light rising on the embankment—
look, Edward, look, a veritable kingdom.

To Baden

"On August 9, 1847, the Spanischbrotlibahn, Switzerland's first railway, made its maiden voyage from nearby Zurich to the great baths of Baden. The railway's nickname comes from a butter-rich pastry so popular that Zurich's 19th-century high society used to send servants either on foot or horseback into the dark to Baden to satisfy late-night cravings. Once the railway was opened, the *spanischbrotli* were delivered by train."   THE BOSTON GLOBE

Into the dark to Baden, then, if need be,
now, or the moment just before, but hurry,
lest mood shift, need diminish, alteration
insinuate its presence, light change, time pass,
education, somewhere, at last, begin,

never looking back, never asking why—
and to what avail, what, to look, to ask,
to know, or hope to know, initiate
an approach to some fixed, ultimate knowledge,
hard-won, if won at all, of what it was,

texture, flavor, the visionary trappings
which set the scene, compose the scene itself,
which may be, once were, are, imaginary,
never, though one might will it otherwise,
part of history, loyal to the fact,

the mind clinging endlessly to its version?:
which of us is to answer, with what words?;
would the language, the phrasing, once discovered,
render moonlight with such fidelity,
depict the depth of woods as dark, as deep?

(the harmlessness, after the fact, assails one:
unthinking cruelties, unspoken wishes,
passion, domesticity, duty, need;
how the footpath may have been plotted, footpaths
too breakneck, too pell-mell, to have been plotted,

improvised, late, quick-as-you-can-be-off-now,
or the lay of the dust in a dry season,
she who lifted her skirts lifting her skirts
that the hems, common muslin stitched belowstairs,
stay unsullied, blinding white, there and back;

what light, should there have been light, struck the angle
at which the rider mounted, cantered, galloped,
head thrust low into night wind, boy's heart pumping
as it never pumped, eyes closed, half-closed, heels jabbed,
over and over jabbing, into flanks

bloodied, soon to be bloodied, in that rage
for time, time, speed, kilometers: oh, pastries!—
what need a young groom know apart from this:
he rides off now on a mission so crucial,
the master has entrusted it to him,

saying, as the boy leaves, Need, need, is all, Hans,
which is enough, whatever it may mean).
The reasons are apparent, or become so,
once the longings of master and of mistress
shall be made known, whispered through servants' quarters,

we from whom they are safe, who shall not judge them,
not peer too closely where we peer, or would peer,
in all their fine complexity their secrets
unraveling, unraveled, now disclosed
(but only after maids and grooms stand pledged—

not a word, swear it, swear, leave this estate—
to silence, feigning ignorance, indifference,
the lassitude ascribed by most to servants,
the sightlessness assumed to be our lot),
the cravings which must flay them, nights, in chambers

sealed to view, once dusk falls, three steep flights up
(architectures persistent yet elusive,
relentless in the way they lash us, haunt us:
where shall their beds be said to lie, their mirrors,
the vanities at which they sit, pose, preen?;

what are the words each whispers in the dark,
that tang of intimacy on the tongue
we would give anything, poor as we are,
bereft ones, drab, nondescript, once to savor,
once, we the common-tongued, untutored, speechless?),

cravings whose names, whose essences, elude us,
as though by name, by name alone, one knew them,
knows them, could have known, hopes to, wholly fails to,
cravings past the imagination servants
are believed to possess, to be possessed by.

Into the dark to Baden, if they must
(no need now, none, to question it: they must),
however odd the hour, whatever weather
befall them on an unmarked route, there, back,
whatever mood seize upstairs maid, manservant,

ordered to leave at once, quick, quick, girl, wake now,
roused perhaps from deep sleep, from dreams of—what?
(who can say what it is the servants dream?);
Marta, time, it is time, such longing flays us
as one cannot depict, and all for pastry;

but be warned, take fair caution: each step, misstep,
skirts disaster, ground shifts, the route meanders,
footing turns treacherous, in due course, worse,
and the delicate, hand-turned crusts, their perfume
carrying through the depth of unmapped woods,

break at a touch, less than that, crumble, shatter,
and the bearer dare not—careful, girl—stumble
where the woods well with darkness leaving Baden,
fragile treasures worth any fortune asked,
worth even those the man shall fail to ask,

fool of a baker, holding in those hands,
alchemist's hands, our ecstasy, our torment,
at the same time—can the magician know?
(infinite kneadings, rich, drenched butterings,
the tenderness of dough worked, rolled, reworked—

tenderness, child, is all, I tell you, all—,
the batters pliant, yielding, worked by fingers
acquiring strength, on and on through the Swiss night,
in the working, reworking: Zurich, breathless,
is waiting, three flights up, on vast estates,

and the fate of the aristocracy,
an empire long dismembered reassembled,
the hunger strike called off, assassinations
in the cabinet canceled, borders closed,
lies in two hands—can the magician know it?):

the margins fluted, just so, edges crimped,
all excess trimmed meticulously, thus,
that the proportions, cakes, crisps, little shortbreads,
those configurations named *spanischbrotli,*
whatever, famished, feverish, one calls them,

endearments not yet coined, whispered, imagined,
be uniform, be sumptuous, be just—
stain upon stain, ring by ring, pools of butter
soaking the bleached-white, dazzling linen napkin
in which the upstairs maids have been instructed

to cradle, with painstaking, utmost caution,
these perfections each, on the way back, clutches—
richness is all, all, more than all, girl, more—,
be worthy of the cravings, nights, of those
lying wracked on silk pillows on estates

where, three flights up, in wings the master plan
neglects to show, obliterates, erases,
gables inflicted at perverse, lost angles,
Zurich, tonight, holding its breath, is dreaming,
learning to suffer, oh, what it most longs for.

(I shall bear them most delicately, Sire,
as deftly as my life, I daresay, more so,
gripping them to my bosom, should I falter.
Fear not, Mistress, I step here with discretion,
though the path is a dark one, long, woods deep,

and the thing craved tenuous past belief.
Trust me, if not to know such need, to sense it,
lowly, dim, poor, not equal to such pangs.
Education is all, Master instructs us,
more than all, should distinctions, this late, matter).

Saddle the horse, Hans: leave, leave now, at once;
someone awaits, in Baden, your arrival.
And should the beast think moonlight in the branches,
swaying seductively, glittering, ghostly,
apples it hopes to pause to sniff, to nuzzle,

sweeter than fruit has any right to be;
should it stray from the path to idle, wander,
wishing (a horse has reasons) to be off now
in pursuit of its own dreams, Hans, not yours
(who can say what it is the horses dream?),

there, where the path turns wild, directionless,
where the meadow verges on incandescence
(any meadow will do, real, imagined)
in some luminous distance, far from Baden;
where the reins, should the rider have forgotten,

just a moment, they were reins he was holding,
the purpose which has brought him here, the mission
on which he rides in frenzy, there and back—
all night, if need be—, all at once go slack,
crowd him in past the dazzle, work the flanks,

insist he move to one idea: Baden,
the ambiguities, in tone, in texture,
of the thing we have agreed to call Baden.
If it is canter suits him, break to gallop;
if it is apples lure him, offer salt.

Teach him what he must learn to live without
(how shall education, Hans, not prove all?);
insist on dreamlessness, domestication,
the long, slow, settling in, the making do.
Whisper in his ear (he will comprehend

nothing of what you say, of course, but you must
hold to words as long as words can be held to)
hunger, craving, appetite, longing, all,
if only, Hans, to keep oneself awake,
responsive to the urgency of missions

on behalf of which you cause flanks to bleed,
or whisper to the creature in the dark
what it is to be needy, stricken, human,
taking this path through woods tonight because
not you nor I know what else one might do.

Baden. Whisper it: Baden. Live for Baden.
It shall sustain the horse as it shall you.
What else is there, this late, to live one's life for,
to know enough to live it for, but this?
(In the end, Hans, shall nothingness prove all?)

I tell you this that you know, know in time,
horses can be made to do anything,
even forget—insist, insist—the past,
whatever past a horse can claim to have,
that past having to do, poor fool, with moonlight

hung from the trees, the confusion with apples,
everything fragrant, lustrous, turned to apples
in his dim mind, apples, once he sniffs woods,
once the magic, the strangeness, overtake him,
the moon dapple his coat, splinter his eye.

Duesenberg, 1929

Speed and light, and what else is one to live for?
The edges rounded, smoothed, attenuated
to the point of imminent disappearance
(where shall speed end and light, at last, begin?),

the givens rearranged, less factual,
less obdurate, than one might have imagined,
once believed might obtain here, must obtain,
the walls guarding the factory abolished—

light, admit light here, let the weather in—,
canceled, revoked, annulled, negated, shattered,
and the words pertaining to the mechanics
of the thing, crankshafts, pistons, axles, gears,

how it "works," unctuous methodologies
of assemblage, construction, piecework, "standards,"
words on the mouths of captain, foreman, workers,
bent at their tasks in narrow, airless places,

words still rancid from usage, common, parched,
stricken, at last, from the vocabularies
of those who, night to night, docile, compliant,
lacking the sense of where roads lead, all roads,

what, on certain evenings, they open out to,
work through the night to meet production schedules
(but for speed, but for light, what shall one live for?;
what, if not embarkation, does one dream of?);

the confines of the drawing board subverted
in favor of—what to call it?—romance,
the utterly chrome-trimmed, the wholly sleek,
that which frees us to follow in its wake,

to improvise, to fill with splendor, grace,
turns, half-turns, cutoffs, dead ends, bends obscured
by all we seem not yet to know about them,
however far they lead, however deep,

the possible lying miles down the road
waiting for someone to have come upon it
late, in a small two-seater, both of us
drenched with the dark, things of pure speed, pure light,

where the road turns, the river, for the first time,
not without effort, each of us pronouncing
names for ourselves, the other, in the dark
names for the dark, for the things one might live for.

On the Plight of Us in the Caravaggio

A detail from *The Sacrifice of Isaac,*
painted by Michelangelo Amerighi da Caravaggio

The decision is made, issues are joined,
the eyes close, one exhales, the body shudders,
night has fallen on Tuscany, the sea
deepens beyond one's concept of it, waves
flail all night on a littoral whose name

need not yet be translated in this poem
nor entered in the book of names, the sixteenth
century cranks its gears, grinds, lumbers on,
and one's place in history is assured,
for the moment at least; there is to be

nothing to stay the rhythm, thwart the blood,
neither the look away nor the turn back,
not reprieve nor the faint hope of reprieve,
neither landscape to save us nor ourselves,
intercessions neither looked to nor asked:

the plot will happen here as it was meant to,
as it must; the queer luster of the blade,
even in half-light, fierce, insidious,
ready, at last, to break into pure flame
or—they come to the same—into pure song,

its supremacy past doubt, beyond reason,
its fervor no mere myth, one's fate no fiction,
seems enough, in the deepest sense, to blind us,
more than enough to implicate us all,
witness, accomplice, murderer, mere painter,

whatever term does proper justice, fits,
collaborators all, bloated with guilt.
The executioner begins to sing
so sweetly it seems not of death he sings.
Isaac is to be sacrificed tonight.

For all the skill implied in the maneuver,
the delicacy crucial to the act,
the darkness sweeping Tuscany, raw fact,
feel the swarthy thumb of the perpetrator
probing the fleshy tissue, sinew, skin,

groping for fleeting comfort, for that spot
by which to hold him through his frenzied thrashing,
past the cries one well knows the boy must cry,
positioning itself astride the cheek
of the pale youth thrown to the cutting block

in the half-tones of an interior
(in Tuscany, all is interior,
drama unfolds indoors, light comes down half-light,
the fire that leaps the grate not yet gone out,
soon to go out, the sheep beyond, the meadow,

imagined, never glimpsed, taken on faith,
the plush brocades draped on the damask cushion
conveying, intricately needlepointed,
all we can know, all we shall ever know,
of sheep in fields, outdoors, life in a province

beyond what dooms, what greens, contend here nightly)
we, in our ignorance, drab, meager, dim,
ascribe to what the painter has us call
the splendors of the sixteenth century;
grappling to find pure bone beneath soft flesh

against which the full hand, but for the thumb
not visible to us, be situated
to do, with no small grace yet with dispatch,
if it were possible, what, from the start,
one knows, one knew, it comes, and soon, to do,

to draw the matter to a close, unravel
plot, take one's fulsome rôle in it, impel
the substantive to resolution, bring
the knife down where the knife should be brought down,
be masterful, fastidious, intent,

for the enlightenment of us, the poor ones,
who may never have glimpsed life past this plain,
nor heard men speak beyond what men speak here,
nor suffered dread, nor dwelled in apprehension
such as that in which one dwells here tonight.

From whatever perspective it falls to us
to view this, paint this, to permit our heads,
with his, interminably to be lowered—
regardless in how agonized a fashion—
to the hard block rich greens conceal throughout,

and in whatever manner one perceives it,
artful, cunning, perverse—choked sob, sigh, whisper:
that dream, each night, of the unspeakable—,
and no matter how sweetly the brute sings
(and the blade with him), longs to sing, however

gorgeous the mauves, the saffrons, the magentas,
playing against our sense of tonal values,
shadows dappling velours, sheens grazing satins,
our fascination with dimension, scale,
from another part of the room a fire

overspilling the grate, flushing its light
through the brocades draped on a damask cushion
painstakingly cross-stitched with antique seed pearls
framing a version of the pastoral
poignant in its resemblance to the "real,"

in a far corner something—the exotic?,
the anguish of the sixteenth century?,
the not-yet-quite-but-soon-to-be-imagined?,
the wholly unimaginable?—glowing,
lit with a light no trappings quite bequeath us,

nor mere accoutrements in fact give rise to;
whatever the distractions, the seductions,
the raging which consumes us at the heart,
it is here we are found, impaled on this:
that, no matter the name, Per, François, Isaac,

however smooth or ravaged the bared flesh,
head pinned, turned, torso twisted, neck crushed, arms locked,
strands of red curls matted to a damp forehead,
the blade comes down, comes down, singing commenceth:
someone is to be sacrificed tonight.

Study the eyes of the boy, head half-turned
on the block by the force the crazed assassin,
under sway of malevolent intent,
looming above, exerts now, brings to bear
as he alone, tonight, can bring to bear,

the weight he has committed to the task
to which he seems too keenly driven, bent,
eyes which, from the angle where he lies jammed,
his position untenable, at best,
the adolescent chest and shoulders, stripped,

glistening with the mist of the boy's sweat,
twitching spasmodically, feverish, clenched,
splayed mercilessly on a scarlet cushion
which, for the moment, quite conceals from view
the cold slab of the cutting block beneath,

look out not at the knife, the fractious blade
seemingly ready to break into song,
to steel itself for song, not at the wretch
who grips the knife so tenderly, so deftly,
with such clear passion for its cut, its line,

the spareness of it all, the utter parchedness,
one would swear the man had been born to coax
music from whatever might lie at hand,
plucked from the grief of evening, wrenched from life,
nothing but music from the bloody knife;

nor to the ten, stray, not-quite-random wisps
of smoke, of brushstroke, lower left-hand corner,
telling us it was Caravaggio,
witness, accomplice, murderer, mere painter,
wracked with unseemly visions, row by row,

in the temples of mauve, saffron, magenta—
the only church to die for, the one god—,
painted this, dreamt this (they come to the same),
made his way through the sixteenth century,
whatever it may or may not have been,

with exemplary courage and blind faith
it was color that mattered, highlight, half-light,
that and such strength as risks making the "real"
one with the dream-struck canvas, leaving them
astonished art should cut so close to life;

but look to you, to you, who stand in wait,
poor, even poorer, still dim, meager, more so,
at the sheer edge, enfabled line, drenched border
where the treacherous, deep frame ends and life,
infinitely more treacherous, begins;

you, as though he thought it were you could turn here,
turn again, change, change again, yield, embrace,
you who could grieve, believe, believe again
it were not yet too late, nor yet too far,
nor the weight past endurance, the dark too dark;

you, to whom it were given to move quickly,
should it not be too late to move at all,
to intercede, to save him, hope to save him,
you who must move, it seems, even more quickly
should it be you, thyself, whom one would save,

the O of the boy's mouth (unuttered cry,
chill of the cutting block, lusters, velours,
murmurings through interiors of damask,
satin's sheen, gasps, brocades) enough to drown in
should one approach incautiously and late,

finding oneself on the brink of the anguish
opening out before us, before him.
Executioner, take thee now to singing:
it were thy blade made music, not thy song.
We are all to be sacrificed tonight.

History, Weather, Loss, the Children, Georgia

"President Franklin D. Roosevelt and his wife, Eleanor,
listening to school children sing in Warm Springs, Ga., 1938."

WIDE WORLD PHOTOS

for Eleanor Taylor

It is a cloudy afternoon in Georgia,
rain predicted to move in by this evening
and to continue through the night till morning.
The clouds are dense, slow-moving, the air sultry,

and the granular texture of the plate,
singular in its unremitting dimness,
a murkiness well past the reach of weather,
beyond intent, design, the dream of art,

past what the picture-taker wished or planned for,
tells us the scene was shot before the advent
of the belief that clarity was all
and the gorgeously shimmering a goal,

the goal, in photographic portraiture,
a time before insistence on deep focus,
the lens which has us see past what the eye sees,
on the angle which makes the most dramatic

statement possible, even though the context
is to be altered, light itself played false,
values rearranged, the view—look—subverted,
suggesting, yet quite subtly, that to see

might be less momentous than how to see,
sightlines, perspective, closure, cropping, frame,
perfections brought to bear for the mere sake of
yet one more haunting afternoon in Georgia.

From the little O's of the children's mouths,
each shaped precisely to accommodate
the unimaginable tenderness,
the utterly uncompromising sweetness,

of the thing that is soon to issue from them,
the song rehearsed, re-rehearsed, through the week,
the highlight of the ceremony scheduled,
one knows a warbling, tentative, elusive,

wandering periodically from pitch,
is to be heard this afternoon in Georgia
(briefly, once, long ago, lost, children, lost)
before the rain carries it all away.

The presidential motorcade, a single
touring car, roofless, driven the few miles
down a gravel road where the summer White House
looms in a grove shadowed by pine and cypress,

is parked before the gray-green clapboard schoolhouse
whose grades have been assembled, first through fifth,
to serenade the President, as promised,
promptly at two-fifteen this afternoon,

the music which they make, soon to rise from them,
should there be music, muted, indistinct,
the sightlines dim, the far perspective cropped,
Georgia distant, receding into myth.

They have tacked a banner to the façade
of the school (Welcome Mister President)
and thrust into the pale, uncertain hands
of three honor students placed in the front row,

expectation flushing their small, plain faces,
three makeshift cardboard placards nailed to slats
perhaps that very morning, when word reached them
visitors, later, were to be expected,

a burden not wholly displeasing to them,
one's guess is, at the same time causing each
vague uneasiness at the sight of cameras,
such prominence all at once thrust upon them,

with no time, this late, to arrange their faces,
rigidity seizing their necks, their spines,
and their eyes, enigmatically evasive,
seeking some haven safer than the lens.

(Movietone News has sent a crew of two —
History Brought to Theatre Screens — to man
two double-spooled machines anchored to tripods,
and we know their faces are to appear,

briefly vulnerable, oh briefly splendid,
Thursday evening, second show, at The Uptown,
light faintly holding, not yet quite extinguished,
between the feature film and the blind juggler,

the little O's, the music teacher's downbeat,
the tune itself anonymous and thin,
fading before it leaks out from the screen;
these and what, throughout, is to come down: weather.)

Two or three men employed by Secret Service
(one guesses at the number since their presence
draws so little attention to itself),
modestly in attendance, unobtrusive,

stand to front and rear of the touring car,
not even thinking, between squinted eyes,
to scan the crowd for malcontents, for plotters,
for the mad or irrational among us,

the disgruntled, for whatever the cause:
these are children gathered to sing, no more,
docile and uncomplaining, without grievance,
well-behaved to a fault, as capable,

girls in round-collared, just-pressed cotton dresses,
boys in freshly starched overalls and white shirts,
of treachery, plots against the Republic,
crimes of subversion, dreams of anarchy,

as you or I that year in Warm Springs, Georgia,
at the side of a road tarred with black gravel,
shadowed, beyond, by clumps of pine and cypress,
grades first through fifth, hushed, patiently awaiting

the music teacher's signal to begin—
thin tunes of unimaginable sweetness
(why is it one is able, stitch by stitch,
garment by garment, to peer at the clothes

in which they were sent off to school that morning
and touch the very heartbreak of the Thirties?),
the day sultry, the sky ominous, burdened,
Mister President waiting to be sung to,

unsmiling but benevolent, forbearing,
the only threat, according to the forecast,
the threat of rain moving in late this evening,
the rest history, myth, the past, the past.

Franklin and Eleanor, beside each other
(geography, proximity, the nature
of the seating arrangements here, not more)
in the rear of this touring car comprising

the motorcade from beginning to end,
sit so contained, so cloaked in privacy
(Eleanor looking cool, despite the weather,
in a pale, long-sleeved, softly draped print fabric

and a flat, black straw hat with grosgrain ribbon
circling the crown whose shade matches the dress),
so parched, so clenched, so obdurate, so final
(Franklin meticulous in his dark suit,

white shirt, a figured tie which falls like silk),
one listens, listens long, one looks, one waits,
for the mere sounds of breathing to escape them,
some last, stray clue these two are drawn from life,

not from The Past, At Last Retrieved, Made Whole,
and Historical Personages Vivid;
and to claim they are seated here together,
with all the resonance the word takes on,

together, though the seat holds two, though two,
from presentiments lurking here, were driven
leisurely down these last, bleached country miles
where the road, two lanes, two, at last gives out

to tar, to gravel, things immensely shadowed,
though two have come to hear the tuneless sing,
and sing for them, he not turning to her,
she not speaking to him, well past the notice

of the children his wholly crucial failure
to reach, say, for her hand, somehow to take it,
to touch her and, in touching, touch himself,
or look, or smile, or once, once, whisper to her

intimacies any man might well whisper
on the brink of the heartbreak of the Thirties
(the voiceless poised to sing, air strangled, sultry,
the music teacher's cue not yet quite given

and the O's not yet having struck their mouths
signaling the insufferable sweetness
of the thing bound, and soon, to issue from them),
would be nothing less than a fabrication.

The Hall, the Hall Grown Cold

Brenda Diana Duff Frazier: "On almost any given night in the late
1930's she could be found perched at the Stork Club with a Camel
clenched in one hand, a champagne glass in the other, and an adoring,
well-bred drone on either side. . . .

"Her social debut was December 27, 1938. The party was held at
The Ritz for two thousand guests. Two bands were engaged and the
entire ballroom suite was rented, in addition to dozens of bedrooms
for exhausted revelers. Despite the flu and terribly swollen feet, Brenda
danced until 6:30 A.M., when Douglas Fairbanks, Jr., draped a tablecloth
around her exposed shoulders. 'Doug said I was shivering, that the hall
must have grown cold,' she later wrote. 'But the hall was not cold at all.
I was shivering from exhaustion.' "   THE PHILADELPHIA INQUIRER

She attempted suicide thirty-one times and spent the last twenty
years of her life in bed.

      The men were like that then, filled with grand gestures,
      the grandest, I might add, imaginable
      to a young girl for whom grandness itself,
      splendor, magnificence, that radiance
      which issues from oneself, seemed foreign countries,
      exotic, half-imagined, out of reach,
      though "filled," of course, will fail to do it justice;
  "swept" cuts closer perhaps, swept with grand gestures,
      a word which could stand, too, for what we were—
      we, the rest of us, those same faces seen
      night to night at the openings, the balls,
      taking up our positions, every evening,
      without fail, on the bar stools, at the tables,
      of what was then "headquarters": yes, The Stork,
      feverish, wracked, impatient, each of us,
      none of us knowing why, none of us asking,
      restless beyond mere mortal restlessness,

being purposeless, strangely, our sole purpose
(our concerns were twofold: that the champagne
would give out, that the band would go home early),
accessories, crucial to no one, nothing,
promising, from one viewpoint, but the promise
of choices wholly failed, connections missed,
false starts, wrong turns, dead ends, untimely entries,
the right moves in the wrong game or, conversely,
the wrong moves in the right game, either one—,
for what the Thirties were, some headlong plunge
to embrace a future none of us dared
think even vaguely of, nor in fact wished to,
summing us as no other chaos sums us.

Think of it: young Doug Fairbanks, hair gold flames,
a smile from here to darkness and beyond,
lithe, dapper, fleet, spilling with energy,
courtly, affectionate, wishing to please,
ready to leap from chandeliers, if need be,
should that, one evening, spare a debutante
awkwardness, pain, embarrassment, distress,
add to whatever grace, whatever beauty,
the moment or the evening might hold for her,
ease her way on the dance floor, turn to glass
the surface on which all night she would glide,
out of what must no doubt have been (I guess this:
how could one have deduced the motivation
impelling others to act out their lives
when one's own life was alien territory?)
nine parts sweet-natured, unselfish concern
to one part, if quite that, boyish bravado
(boredom, exuberance, intoxication
of midnight come and gone, of girls in ballgowns,
whiffs of perfume, corsages, night to night
the fashionable aimlessness of evenings
spent here, spent there, what did it matter?, elsewhere,

spent anywhere, whatever the address,
yet, as one comes to understand, spent nowhere),
thinking to seize, confronted all at once
with the girl's plight, not a chinchilla stole
from its ebony hanger on the rack
where the attendant dozes in the cloakroom,
to snatch not a blue marten evening cape,
not a pearl-encrusted angora wrap,
from a girl in the vestibule who lingers
far too long over her Good Nights, Good Nights,
nor yet quite bring himself to ask her escort
momentarily to surrender his
meticulously tailored dinner jacket
faced with monogrammed silk, its lapels satin,
to drape about the shoulders of Miss Frazier,
Brenda, shivering, under those revolving
blue pinhead spots, star-shaped, set in the ceiling—
our faces moonlit, starlit, ghostly, passing
in and out of vague shadows as we danced—
of a ballroom already half-abandoned
to that semidarkness crowding the Thirties
relentlessly (who among us had noticed?),
but, instead, from a now-deserted table,
lime parfaits melting, melted, in their goblets,
cigarette stubs floating in demitasse cups,
linen napkins crumpled in finger bowls,
a single satin evening slipper, silver,
tassels forlorn, bedraggled, propped beneath
a chair (misplaced?, abandoned?, left behind?),
seizing its damask cloth—a moment of
high drama—, whipping it across the air,
sending to the floor silver, crystal, china
(the crash that could be heard as far as Wall Street),
drawing the fabric tight across my shoulders,
gently closing its folds, fold upon fold,
in the belief, dear Doug, I had grown cold,

having danced so long, so late, into darkness,
and with so many partners, each so nimble,
so gracious, so compliant, one lost count
as the evening progressed and, slowly, slowly,
the band had, tune by tune, quite as intended,
accomplished what it had set out to do:
cause us to forget ourselves, time, the Thirties,
our place, our very placelessness, within them,
forget the cold, the hall grown cold, that ballroom
at The Ritz (was it waking, was it sleeping?;
where might the border lie?), whose constellations,
lovely blue spots recessed into the ceiling,
all night slowly revolved above our heads,
stippling our faces, shadows stalked by shadows,
nothing, nothing whatever (knowledge come by
later, perhaps too late), enough to save us
from waking or from sleeping, nothing, nothing,
which might have helped us tell one from the other,
nothing, nothing whatever, which, in time,
might have enabled us to live, might, once, have
shown us, nothing whatever, what to live for.

Here I am looking up at Geer T. Garrow,
Geer every bit as beautiful as I:
dark hair, dark eyes, lovely patrician features—
such an elegant young man, so well turned out,
the long, thin nose, the fine mouth, perfect stock
for breeding, as one's forebears might have put it,
and no doubt did, all the while scrutinizing
aspects of lineage, studying bloodlines,
the prospect of vast fortunes to be merged,
of empires—oil, steel, coal—consolidated.
How enthralled I seem to be, how adoring
the gaze is, undeflected; those eyes focus
as they focused on little in the Thirties,
with a purity, an intensity,

which even now, this late, though I remember
nothing of the young man, of what I felt,
of what I failed to feel (this seems more likely),
has the power, even now, now, to shock me,
even now, even now, astonishes me,
moves me for what it gives me of myself
as it addresses, half addresses, longing
(what is it, name it, once, just once, I longed for,
might have longed for, had the gift, once, to long for?;
specify, localize, narrow the range:
was the name of it waking, was it sleeping?),
mirrors, recalls, redeems, returns in fragments,
for what it fails, the larger part, to give me.

Study her eyes, her gaze, note her expression:
oh, how enthralled, how filled with adoration,
she is, or was, or could have been, or might be,
Brenda standing there gazing up at Geer
as though in that brief gaze, summed, fixed, complete,
after all these decades unchanged, unchanging,
lay the end and beginning of all gazing,
Brenda holding a cocktail in one hand,
that year's chic cocktail, no doubt (name forgotten,
recipe lost, with the rest of it), Brenda
with that grotesque corsage snaking its way—
gardenias, whose fumes sickened her all evening—
down the bodice and shoulder of a gown
it took, it might have taken, seventeen
fittings to fashion to the right proportions,
seventeen, count them, just so, in a style
deemed to be, to have been, that year's smart style,
smartest style, fabric clinging to the waist,
softly, subtly, shirred at the bosom, grazing,
barely grazing, the young girl's shapely ankle
at the hemline, above her satin slipper,
a hue chosen to flatter hair, eyes, skin tone,

its highlights, all night, magical, refracting,
showing her, throughout, to her best advantage,
nothing overlooked, nothing (destinies
hang in the balance, each night, on one's prospects,
remember, on the "catch" one makes, may yet make,
the one which—lumber?, cattle?—just escapes)—
patience, Brenda, Miss M's exquisite needle
must baste a moment longer, then: perfection!

This photograph was taken at The Met
where, in the Thirties, one had to be seen
should she hope to present the right credentials,
to prepare for "the future," to establish
the basis of an authenticity
nowhere else as plausible, as unquestioned.
There were those who passed judgment on such matters:
one's position, one's right to that position,
could be confirmed or denied in a stroke;
one's presence at the opera, charities, balls,
any one of a hundred "worthy causes,"
should one have youth and beauty on one's side,
lent one the weight one might otherwise lack.
It was "weight" one needed to marry "right."
All that was required of debutantes
was that they be beautiful and "appear":
"appearing" may have been what I did best,
the only thing, in fact, as I recall.
One need do nothing else, the rest would follow.

What can he be saying that holds me, held me
(enchantment reigns this evening at The Met;
what the magic was onstage hardly matters),
or could it be he says nothing at all,
nothing, needs to say nothing, stands there mute,
himself, Geer T., whoever that may be,
may have been, youthful, bright-eyed, tall, erect

(to locate him is to locate oneself),
hope, the last hope, of a long line of Garrows,
one, it seems, more resplendent than the next,
each as powerless to affect the future
as Geer himself must have been, I no less so,
in need no longer of vocabulary
(somewhere we turn into ourselves, embody
definition, disappear into syntax,
our own—pure, deep, fierce, fixed, for all time fixed),
needing only to stand there as he stands,
paragon, icon, symbol, end, beginning,
innocent, calm, wholly exemplary,
yet so touched by a pathos, a foreboding,
never explained, never explainable,
the sense of something soon, too soon, to fall,
it breaks the heart to gaze into his face,
freshly shaved for the opera, for his date
with the dark-haired debutante of the year
(of the century, some no doubt would claim)—
Brenda, seen only last night at The Stork,
young men, to right, to left, forming a line
for the privilege of lighting her Camel,
the night before, her debut, at The Ritz,
under revolving pinhead lights, all blue
(was the name of it waking, was it sleeping?),
studding the ceiling to immense effect,
casting shadows, star-shaped, across their faces
(the magic passing onstage hardly mattered),
trailing their steps where, dance by dance, they step,
Doug Fairbanks (kind?, gallant?, misguided?, foolish?)
suddenly draping her, arms, bosom, shoulders,
in a welter of dazzling table linen—
drama implicit everywhere, grand gestures—,
cascade after cascade, fold upon fold
(folly?, delusion?, daydream?, nightmare?, vision?;
the hall, dear Doug, the hall, the hall grown cold),

Geer's hair sleek, still damp, the youth's dinner jacket
betraying, through the Thirties, not a crease,
not a flaw, where he sits, stands, dips, bends, partners,
as though his clothing had been occupied
intermittently, and then barely, briefly,
Geer smiling, face upturned, as perishable
as I beneath these lights at intermission
(what they were singing onstage hardly mattered)
catching us in their crossfire between acts,
these echoes (distant, faint now, faint), these auras,
Geer, no less purposeless, it can be certain,
going to meet the Forties, having left,
or soon to leave, the Thirties just last evening,
or the evening before that (waking?, sleeping?) —

ordering drinks at The Stork, the long bar
crowded with the same faces, Thirties' faces,
youthful, beautiful, smiling, bored, soon, too soon,
darkened, most of them, by what (soon, too soon)
seems bound to overtake them; in a hansom
smelling too much of fresh paint for one's comfort
(the marks beneath two coats not quite contained,
as intended, overrunning their borders,
the painted-over visible, insistent),
too angular, too narrow, too lopsided,
to negotiate all it must this evening,
whose driver sports a silk top hat shades blacker
than the dark through which he must drive the horse,
a horse, fitted with blinders, all night tracing,
circle by circle, the maze of the park,
seeming not to find a way out or back;
in the ballroom of The Ritz—decorations
in place, corsages pinned (shoulders, wrists, waists),
ballgowns, basted in time, tucked, straightened, smoothed,
coiffures adjusted, long, last looks in backstage
dressing-room mirrors, nothing overlooked,

nothing, necklaces fastened, bracelets clasped,
the band launching into Gershwin, Cole Porter,
couples drifting to the terrace, excitement
building, building, palpable—where Miss Frazier,
debutante of the year, Brenda herself,
Miss Glitter, Miss Amazing, Miss Rich Catch,
is to make her debut, is to "appear,"
has, in fact, already "appeared," seen dancing
so many dances, with so many partners,
so many hours since the ball began,
since the Thirties pronounced, or sealed, their fates,
one loses count of dances, partners, hours,
loses a sense of decades necessary
for the comprehension of history,
loses even the reason Doug, Doug Fairbanks
(swaggerer?, dreamer?, charmer?, bungler?, prankster?),
catching a glimpse of her across the dance floor
under a shower of blue pinhead lights,
starry and dreamlike (was it waking?, sleeping?;
find the name for it, once, once, mark the border),
noting the broken rhythm, the blind steps,
seeing her shoulders quiver, her arms shake,
fearful her faltering, her hesitation,
signaled the loss of all control, the failure
of success, the tarnishing of all beauty,
thought the girl cold (the hall, dear Doug, the hall),
moved to do what a gentleman must do,
six in the morning, Brenda shivering,
breathless, fatigued, limp, pale, stopped, at a loss,
the ball at an end, nearly at an end,
the wraps retrieved, the cloakroom girl gone home,
the band dispersed, the splits of champagne emptied,
the lights dimmed, the blue pinhead star-shapes gutted,
the Thirties (waking?, sleeping?: give its name),
by the time day breaks, overturned, the Forties,
The Stork deserted, horses pulling hansoms

(how many coats, how many—slick, black coats—,
will it take to disguise the vehicle,
to conceal what it served to draw before this?)
with all the strength at their command still finding
no way out, no way back, deep in the park
(how many coats?), the hall grown cold, grown colder,
the guests asleep in upstairs suites, Doug, dear Doug,
swept with grand gestures, their true master, draping
the debutante in table linen, making
light, in the dark, of what he does, yet doing
all he can do, all anyone can do,
to intervene, to warn her, warm her, save her.

Approaching a City

for Lynda Hull

Dear Mr. Hopper,
                    It was just this morning
(why should it seem I have felt all I feel
from the beginning, though I cannot date it,
as though, even before seeing your painting,
even before I knew that I must write you,
I knew whatever I would come to know,
even the manner I would come to know it?)
Mrs. Carmody led us on a tour—
"impartial, though I cannot be expected
not to be human, not have personal favorites"—
through the gallery (light from all directions,
where we would turn, would not yet turn, light spilling
to the paintings themselves, across what Mrs.
Carmody, "though I hesitate to call it
what it requires I call it," calls "the trap
of brutal, obscure corners, corners telling
as much about themselves as about us,
as about Edward Hopper, corners bearing
their secrets almost proudly, if not proudly,
with an uncommon passion," which each canvas
can be said to possess, or be possessed by—
of necessity, Mrs. C would claim—,
"corners from which one extricates oneself
not easily or soon, as one would want it,"
the floors, superbly polished, glinting, buffed,
their sheen enough to skate on, each refracting
light pouring from high windows, portholes, fanlights,
halls endlessly turning this way, or that,

endlessly burrowing deeper and deeper
into that maze of vision, complication,
astonishment, awaiting us on walls
ending, just before noon, in a cramped lobby,
a niche, adjacent to a vestibule,
off to one side, easily overlooked
were it not for the nine capital letters,
fittingly emblematic, which the sign bears—
omen?, warning?, hint of what is to come
in a world where little is known, less given,
where there are damages to be reported?—,
nine bold letters in stark relief emblazoned,
stenciled across the lintel: FINAL EXIT)
where, from what seems nothing less than sheer wisdom,
they have taken it on themselves to hang
that mysterious dreamscape, burdened, haunted,
pinned to its canvas by the unexplained,
to which you have attached the name Approaching
a City, now compelling me to write
in terms you and I shall have understood,
by the end of this letter, not at all,
or at least not enough to make worthwhile
the effort to be put into the reading.
(There are damages here to be reported,
damages which the mind cannot begin
even to weigh, to estimate, to name.)

It is now I must write this, Mr. Hopper,
now I need to begin, before it fades,
dissipates, vanishes, drifts off to smoke
(a fitting image, as becomes apparent),
before whatever sense one shall have made
lies too scattered, too late, at last, to make
what Mrs. Carmody suggests I put down
even if only for that sense of self
unique to each of us, no more, just that,

on behalf of what clarity, what light,
it may lend to one's own—her word—"perspective,"
though, of course, it shall not enlarge your own,
you whom these words shall leave just as you were,
unchanged, unmoved, perhaps not moved enough,
at a time you were unaware a student,
changed by your painting, moved more than he knew,
would write to you from ignorance, from need,
from that unholy ground where the two meet.

Before leaving the gallery this morning,
our little tour concluded, one more lesson
in art appreciation at an end
(if not, dear Mrs. Carmody, instruction
in how, at last, to see, or what to live for),
the lobby jammed with other tours and students,
having seen all that they had come to see,
one or two having seen, no doubt, much more,
what, in fact, some had never come to see
(there are damages here to be reported),
arranging us in double matching rows,
apportioned just so, perfectly aligned,
one exactly duplicating the other,
undeviating, orderly, precise,
sight lines pleasing, perspectives shapely, clear,
an artist's eye plotting the whole deployment,
counting to see no one was left behind,
no one dawdled before a favored painting,
lingered admiring shading, angle, scale,
marveling at the quality of brushstrokes,
their subtlety, their depth, sheer understatement
trailing off into whispers, evanescence,
at the utter absence of "decoration,"
tonal values wholly in contradiction,
juxtapositions playing off one shade
uncannily against another, each one,

citron, persimmon, lime, mauve, beige, magenta,
unresolved in the background, each small balance
won, for the moment, soon, all too soon, lost,
restive, unquiet, charged, disruptive, drenched
with a drama of unbearable tension
nowhere defined, nowhere definable,
Mrs. Carmody told us we might purchase
a postcard version of that work of art
which spoke most intimately to us, moved us,
moved us deeply, one to a student, even
may have changed us, "though you shall not yet know that,"
"just to ponder, to study, just to hold to,
later, a moment longer," that one painting
"it may become your joy, even your terror,
those who are the fortunate ones among you,
the ones arriving singularly gifted,
to be unable, as you soon discover—
tomorrow, the day after, a slow learning,
admittedly, an anguish, a climb upward—,
utterly unable, to live without."
Most of the others, less fixed from the start
("doomed," perhaps, is the word one might have written),
seem to have had some difficulty choosing
which of two or three works they wished to ponder
(study, hold to, live with, attempt to live with),
unlike myself, immediately drawn,
drawn and held, I should tell you, Mr. Hopper,
fatally drawn, perhaps, fatally held,
to the one I am holding here before me
this evening, as I write this, darkness falling,
the one with damages to be reported
beyond the mind to weigh, estimate, name.

It is yours I had chosen, knew I must choose,
yours I ponder, study, begin to live with,
begin, I should say, to attempt to live with

(a long, slow learning, as had been predicted,
more than an anguish, more than a climb upward,
more than anything which might be said of it),
brooding beneath the lamp where I have propped it,
ready, from the evidence, more than ready—
how shall I put this?—to break into flames,
wanting it here before me as I write this,
wanting it haunted, burdened, still amazing,
unforgettable, vivid, unforgotten,
significations spilling from it, omens,
hoping, in time, somehow to make sense of it
(or to make peace with it, which is the same),
even the dimmest, yet not too much sense,
needing to see as fiercely as I can
yet not enough, perhaps, to see too clearly,
that imprecision not quite wholly blind me
to those deeper strangenesses lodged within it.
Knowing neither what my "gifts" are, or may be,
what, tomorrow, I may arrive endowed with
("the ones arriving singularly gifted"),
whether I am, or was, or one day shall be,
for no reason apparent, no just cause,
at risk of turning, slow, dim, unprepared,
inarticulate, seeing not too clearly,
into one of the fabled "fortunate ones,"
I find myself unable, Mr. Hopper,
"utterly unable," to live without
this City of yours, this now mythic City,
ineffable, inevitable, both,
City the maps refuse to chart precisely,
City we make our way to, nameless, placeless,
if not quite back from, darkness falling, fallen
("the trap," she said, "of brutal, obscure corners,"
extrication not simple and not soon,
if at all possible, as you devise it),
you seem, and shall remain forever seeming,

in process (Mrs. C might say "a learning"),
arduous, weighted, long, more than an anguish,
more than a mere climb upward, of Approaching.

I see those rows of windows, row on row,
you wish us to believe compose a city,
tenements lining some bleak gutted street
trailing off into twilight's distant suburb,
nothingness, hush, faint whisper, murmur, echo,
the ache of what one knows will not avail,
at the back of the mind, if even there
(shall it be said that others live here, witness
the fall of darkness, evenings, in the dark
tremble, know longing, dream, remember, cry out?),
windows whose curse, whose burden, whose affliction,
unspeakable and eloquent at once,
is, as you have arranged it, Mr. Hopper,
to seem to look not out nor to look in
(when I think of the cost to you, I shudder),
blind windows on a back street nameless, placeless,
in a City—each least detail withheld,
those not withheld magnificently garbled,
those not yet garbled falsified, invented,
those not invented no doubt soon invented,
the map, should there be maps, needing revision,
canceled, revoked, outdated, superseded,
no use whatever to us on a journey
whose hope, whose dream, was to be logical
(no longer the thing hoped for, the thing dreamt),
latitude, season, weather, undisclosed,
our sense of the terrain, geography's
subtleties, certainties, resplendent magic,
lost on us here, late, too late, unredeeming,
outrageously deceptive, fabrications—
it is, it has become, our task, our fate,
to be, without reprieve or intercession,

in however circuitous a fashion
(think of the cost, the toll exacted; shudder),
forever in the process of Approaching—
no more, just that, that alone, mere approach,
not even an advance on, say, the core,
where the City itself lies, the lives in it,
feverish, weathered, glinting, struck, impassioned,
the setting out obscured, the route not straight,
the light too dim, the dark not bright enough,
the damages unspeakable, at best,
more extensive, it happens, than imagined,
destinations unmarked, even if marked
mismarked, misleading, fraudulently promised,
impossible to reach, to reach in time,
to reach where reaching would at last avail,
before the thing to be attained prove wholly
unattainable (how are we to know it
when we arrive there?, what small recognition
is to be granted?, what hint, what admission,
of vision, omen, flame, signification;
in the end this, this, too: how to pronounce it?,
by what name shall it ask that it be called?).
Why should those windows, window after window,
looking not out nor in from blind façades,
overwhelm us with the utterly futile,
the terror of the too symmetrical,
perched high above the cut where tunnel diggers,
hammering day and night, anonymous
(how many seasons, what year, in what weather?),
each with a history unknown to us,
blasted a viaduct that tracks be laid
between the here and there, even approaching
the city, fabled, far, of one's own strangeness?

The thing that breaks the heart, at last, or would,
or soon seems destined to, upon reflection,

will be those murky smudges splayed on concrete,
overhead, where the train enters the tunnel
(where, at least, one assumes trains enter tunnels),
arriving and departing every evening
as trains never have and yet always shall,
keeping quite scrupulously to a schedule
obsolete by the time one seeks connections—
for just how many years is it now, tell me;
one loses count, needs, of course, to lose count—,
several mud-brown brushstrokes artfully
arranged not to seem artfully arranged,
little soot marks smoke has left where the engine
slows on the downgrade near the viaduct
(all progress, any progress, being progress
into the tracklessness of one's own strangeness),
their true color bled from them, toneless, muted
to the brink of imminent disappearance
(a small detail, admittedly, yet one
so touched with grace, with anguish, so unasked-for,
so contained in the cry it would cry out,
so consistent with the vision presented,
so much a piece with the rest, with the silence
welling from windows, tenements, with tunnels
waiting for trains one knows will never come,
never keep quite scrupulously to schedule,
with namelessness, with placelessness, with darkness
forever falling here, never quite fallen
("corners bearing their secrets almost proudly"),
one shall not search beyond it for, say, "meaning"—
no need to ask the artist what he "meant,"
Mrs. C tells us; "he is last to know")—,
nearly an inadvertence on your part,
it would seem, Mr. Hopper, but not quite,
painted as flat, as dry, as unobtrusive
as paint and brush and thinner hope to make them,
discoloration, living stain, the mark

of weather having come and having gone,
passing through suburbs resolutely nameless,
leaving us as we were, as we shall be,
weatherless, timeless, parched, in a dry season
knowing no year, no border, no reprieve,
pale smoke of engines rising as the railbed
leads the train deeper, deeper, underground
and the view closes in on implication,
where all trace of the local, the express,
the in-betweens long since dropped from the schedule,
once passing here, once stopping, once departing,
once partaking of all that trains partook,
clamor, fever, passion of embarkation,
will have been quite effectively erased,
obliterated, turned, in fact, to smoke—

a little thing, perhaps, a final stroke,
coda, footnote, finishing touch, summation,
minor and wayward, random, fragmentary,
not meant to be more than last-minute, yet
crucial to vision, to what one would see,
delicate and detailed, caring enough,
even meticulous enough, to wrench us
back to the look of the approach, the look
of suburbs which lead, must lead, either way—
into, out of, neither, both—, the look
of whatever burns itself in the mind
and stays, retained, contained, held long, held fiercely,
all things tenuous, late, beleaguered, scorched,
intended to be no more than passed over
in a glance, in a word ("appreciation,"
museum tours, lessons in how to see,
in what, at last, to live for, unavailing,
despite your efforts, Mrs. C), the look,
even, of approaching a city for which
there is no name, there never was a name

(all names proving, in the end, dispossessions),
there may not even have been an approach
(there are damages here to be reported,
Mrs. Carmody might have warned, but failed to),
yet a city we seem destined to know,
know at once (the fortunate ones among us,
those of us marked as singularly gifted),
one it seems our fate is not to mistake,
even in a failed season such as this,
misjudge the nature of, the distance to,
however bleak, ungainly, slow, our progress
in reaching some accommodation with it,
not see clearly (though in conformity
with those principles earlier established,
one might wish not too clearly, Mr. Hopper),
nor understand the vein of desolation
from which the stones that pave these streets are mined,
that front the blind façades above the cut
where, downgrade, downgrade, trains take to the tunnel
as they always have and yet never shall,
where each of us grows now a little darker
in the evening, beneath the viaduct
(there are damages here still unreported),
discoloration, weather mark, time stain,
and the heart comes to know, at last, what breaks it.

Joyce on the French Coast
Waiting for the Dark

Though one should not know too soon what he waits for,
what the posture implies, should not surmise
the precise music with which the man struggles,
in which we find him, coming late here, locked,
turning his back to the fierce ravishments

of sky, of surf, of the French littoral,
nor understand too easily three youths
on their flight south, the oddness of the angle
at which, this evening, they approach the camera,
only to glance off, left, out of the picture,

should the time come, assume who they may be,
into what lives each, grown, complex, might flee,
nor name, if speak at all, definitively
landscapes we alone are left to determine
which are imaginary, which are real,

Joyce sits, at twilight, in a field of wild grass,
darkness gathering, gathered, holds his head
in hands delicate, slender, almost fragile
(time to pause, rest, be still, dream, wait for music),
his palms cupping both ears as he looks down,

black patch sealing one eye, the other closed,
an ascot, white, draped loosely at the neck,
tucked with no thought to style beneath the collar
where shirt gives way to languid, half-tied knot,
its sleeves ending just above Joyce's wrists,

three buttons gleaming softly at each cuff,
his trousers (muslin?, linen?) baggy, crumpled,
after what must have been a long day's outing,
starting early, making progress, if any,
hesitantly, across this dry, flat plain

meant, we are told, to stand for the French coast
(if not yet told, destined soon to be told),
the southern coast, further disclosure has it,
though there is no map to prove or disprove it,
all of it mere conjecture at this point,

speculation in the gathering darkness,
what, throughout, we resist having defined,
the route made too explicit, the Cape named,
located too precisely: give the moment,
give Joyce himself, the freedom to elude us.

Then there are boys, three boys, in silhouette,
their faces indistinct yet lustrous, joyous,
advancing by degrees from the left, rear,
breaking into the steps of a slow gallop
both serene and high-spirited at once,

as they cross, or attempt to cross, this field,
this meadow which one takes on faith as France,
that coast where Joyce sits, once sat, as described,
their stride here tender, buoyant, strangely weightless,
making small noise, if any, little clamor,

as the photograph shows them closing in,
slowly, inexorably, twilight weather,
just above the tenuous definition,
in the half-light, of Joyce's dim left shoulder—
itself quite enigmatic where the coastline

billows, lifts seaward, yielding Cap d'Antibes
(Cap-Ferrat?, Castillon?, La Seyne-sur-Mer?),
could one have looked, looked up, glanced left, right, glimpsed
those features one might call distinguishing,
rocky spit, salt flat, cove, nine cypresses

in a row, scrupulously at attention,
anything but this darkness coming down,
this namelessness in the center of which
Joyce sits, once sat, head in hands, waits, the coast
nowhere identifiable, yet French.

The youngest in the middle, his companions
joining hands with him, flank to splendid flank,
brows radiant, cheeks flushed, faint perspiration
highlighting rims of noses, hairlines, chins,
their health so manifest, fixed, unrelenting,

they come at us at such calm, steady pace,
utterly dreamlike, fabulous, unrushed,
no more than a vague flurry of the wind,
Joyce can hardly have heard them as they tracked
south-by-southeast, on the diagonal,

the course they take almost certain to take them
out of the frame containing him completely,
and the author, with one eye closed, one patched,
seeing, at the same time, nothing and all,
lulled by whatever dream, at dusk, he dreams,

gripped by essential music, phrase by phrase,
measure for measure, rapt, immersed, transfixed,
dissonances perverse, extreme, complex,
stripped of everything on this alien coast
but what matters, oneself, one's strangeness, weather,

French grasses splayed before him wave on wave
cushioning what small cries each, soaring, makes,
might have made, boys in flight, three boys, ecstatic,
may have thought it was wind, mere, random flurry,
rising behind him, crossing south-by-southeast,

rather than these three on the French coast, children
veering off at an angle bound to take them
wholly out of the author's field of vision,
past the range of his hearing, three youths running
breakneck and pell-mell inland from the sea,

what one takes as the sea, sweat-soaked, resplendent,
where, as we knew from the start, his hands pressing
fiercely against the ears, one of the eyes shut,
refusing its distractions, one eye gutted,
wounded beyond what words might make it see,

Joyce in a surf of grasses in a meadow,
we agree, for want of a better fiction,
to call, merely provisionally, French,
lost to himself, to music, gripped by myth,
all of it shall utterly have escaped him.

Almost precisely counterbalancing
the children in their sector (grass field, left),
the weight three boys, ecstatic, have displaced,
might yet displace, should the tale be unraveled,
should the imagined turn, in time, to fact,

on the verge between middleground and background,
borders tenuous, wavering, in doubt,
Joyce unaware of multiple distinctions
being made where the dark falls, long since made
(how are we to say where pure field begins

and the rest of it, dreaming, myth, leaves off?,
tell where, at last, three boys, nameless, soon faceless,
outpace what dogs their heels here, the ecstatic?,
know what to claim as Joyce, even as Joyce's,
to differentiate it from the dark?),

hands jamming ears, eyes shut, flayed by French grasses,
sailing out on that music he alone hears,
there looms a speck, no more, on the horizon,
unconfirmed, arbitrary, coastal rumor,
shadow, blur, photographic imperfection

(flaw in the proof, scratch on the negative,
distortion in the lens, grain of dust, sand,
pale strand of what may have been human hair
violating a so-called perfect view,
overexposure, marring of the plate),

what we dream is a dory—look—, envision
as a vessel well-crafted, deep, seaworthy,
stout-timbered where the prow must part the sea,
ready for embarkation, voyage, something
in which, at last, the children might make landfall—

the signs propitious, kind, the weather coastal,
given a sail, a sea, the first stars rising
as they rise nowhere but on this French coast—,
despite its flimsiness, its visionary
quality in the moonlight, half-seen, unseen,

from which these boys, three boys, long past their flight
down the French coast tonight, may or may not
make fables of which myth, dream, may consist,
should they have paused to glance, first left, then right,
look for blue waves on a gray, placid sea,

peer for sails on a dory nameless, sail-less,
here where even the dory lies in question,
even, years later, could they have remembered
a sprint on the diagonal, ecstatic,
removing them from the deep frame completely,

wonder whether it had, in fact, been Joyce,
Joyce at the edge, in dry grass, Joyce uniquely
positioned to hear nothing, to see nothing,
lost to music, to grasses, strangeness, self,
lost to whatever it is one is lost

where one waits on the coast of France, lost even
to the whispered name of the fabled port
where the youths, three youths, had there been a dory
riding it out a kilometer offshore,
the flaw on this expanse of dim, gray water,

the speck, the scratch, the blur, the human hair,
all things we say it is which it is not,
had the dory sported a hand-turned sail,
luminescent, fabulous, sheer white, blinding,
and the sail had a French wind tugging at it,

tacking due south to Cap d'Antibes, beyond,
those other capes which still await their names,
might, in true sailing weather, flee their context,
escape the frame, articulate a landfall
fitting and just, momentous, yet elusive,

the vessel timbers, nails, vague, nondescript,
but the boys, these three children, running slant,
beautiful, damp-browed, breathless, gleeful, hushed,
Joyce to the rear, the side, head bowed, late, lost,
waiting for music, drenched, rapt in the frame.

Opera

Mother sits in the back seat lulled by Verdi,
I beside her, the winter I am seven,
the Rockaways, Father has us believe,
our destination, for a glimpse of the sea,

though we have seen the sea before, my brother
and I, if not yet to the degree Father
would have us see—light, lights, half-lights, gradations—,
sufficiently for us to cry "the sea,"

two boys, seven and twelve, who, having followed
Father headlong in pursuit of routes south,
south, always south, smell the Bay, cross the causeway,
are at last, blinded, stunned, made to confront it.

Father has memorized each rise, each turn,
knows them by heart, as my brother does, too,
it seems, seated as he is in the front seat
with a view of what opens out before us,

I, in what would seem, on the surface, a less
advantageous position, with a view
not as inclusive, car-bound, but, despite that,
bearing an intensity quite beyond

what the mere fact, for all its worth, attests to,
an interior view, one might describe it.
(Why did I not believe, even now fail to,
Rockaway, as claimed, was our destination:

was it likely, possible, all that sky,
all those deep routes opening out before us,
all the fervor of that daylong pursuit,
all that light, all those lights, half-lights, gradations,

deliver us to this, not more than this,
three syllables too composed, too domestic,
to bear us south to the fierce, the exotic,
lacking the least frail light, lights, necessary?)

Mother, in the back seat, hums Donizetti.
It is cold in the car. I sit beside her
nuzzling the gray fox collar of her coat,
asleep, or half-asleep, or merely dreaming

(voyages into life, my life, the music
lying in wait where music lies in wait,
where one senses music must lie in wait),
those voices sweeping to us from Manhattan,

wave on wave, at full tide, breaking across us,
mezzo-soprano after mezzo-soprano,
one outpacing the other, teaching us
how to live, what to suffer, moving us

in ways we thought, once, we could not be moved,
the car robe tucked and folded in our laps,
blue, like the car, one side faced with soft wool,
the other with smooth Russian karakul

whose knack it is, or was, or always shall be,
to catch the light of each bleached scene we pass through,
light, lights, half-lights, the infinite gradations,
highway, field, causeway, marshland, swampflat, beach,

in a far corner, bold yet modest, quiet,
neither self-effacing nor prepossessing,
an emblem of the same blue, sea-blue, wool,
embossed to shape a circle, duplicating

the initials Mother and Father both share,
an intricate, elaborate nest of scrolls,
inordinately difficult to follow,
from which it seems there shall be no escape,

yet, in a resolution near the border,
curlicues signifying, somewhere, ends
(or beginnings—one cannot yet know which)
neither looked to nor hoped for, unexpected,

fretwork coming, at last, into its own,
worked and reworked, the way cleared, almost cleared,
if not yet cleared, clearing, soon to be cleared,
flowering into something evident,

apparent, from the most hidden of sources,
burdened with complication, breaking into
the most magnificent lucidity
imaginable, all at once made plain,

plainer than plain, ultimate, beautiful,
serene (worked and reworked, done, undone, cleared),
an appliqué-on-appliqué the fingers
of a boy, seven that winter, seem not to

have enough of, never to have enough of,
never tire of tracing, then retracing,
BM, the circle rounded, BM, BM,
circle reversed, circle rounded, BM,

on and on through a winter afternoon
dazzling with light, with expectation, promise
(the sun makes it seem ice hangs from the trees),
all the way to the Rockaways, beyond,

the Atlantic, still miles south, not yet sighted
(never, perhaps, fable that it is, sighted),
Father and my brother in the front seat,
maps spread between them, views, speed, mileage, motion,

Mother in fox, the car robe tucked about us,
Claudia Muzio's voice filling the car,
instructing us in some romantic anguish
both unforgettable and undeciphered,

hinted at, dimly glimpsed, not yet spelled out—
music lying in wait for us?, the sea
Father insists lies south, due south?, one's life?—,
that scene least fathomed, least definitive.

It shall not matter that this is the year
gas is rationed, that pale green books of coupons
are to be surrendered, gallon by gallon,
that station after station has been shuttered,

one by one stricken, mute, the length of Broadway,
toppled by forces (plague?, contamination?)
hardly comprehended by a boy, seven;
that chains of mail are strung across each driveway

barring entry to the pumps, to the lifts,
to the depths of those bottomless enclosures
where the dark seems to well at its profoundest,
signs spelling LUBRICATION PITS effaced.

The car fills now with Don José, with Carmen.
Lily Pons breaks the heart, should one permit her.
(One has no qualms whatever acquiescing.)
Mother, in fox, tucks the car robe about me,

gently, securely, softly croons Bizet.
It is both cold and warm here in the car,
the cold explainable, if not the warm.
Mother launches into the Habanera.

Father, it seems, has little taste for opera,
my brother less. I think the route consumes them,
specific routes, specific destinations
("the Rockaways"), mileage, distance, direction,

the turns to take, not take, marks on the map,
tomorrow visible on the horizon
rather than intimated. It may be
precisely intimation I most savor,

the barely seen, the half-seen, the unseen,
the scene least fathomed, least definitive,
the possible lying in wait, like music,
in a direction neither specified

nor specifiable on the bright map
Father and my brother have spread between them
on the front seat, the glimpse beyond all glimpses,
the note beyond the notes denoting "opera,"

what Puccini, even now, even now,
as we race to the Rockaways, beyond,
a thousand miles from nowhere, drunk on light,
the route at last coming into its own,

worked and reworked, the way cleared, almost cleared,
a whiff of salt, of surf, still in the distance,
one's life lying in wait where a life waits,
has been struggling, throughout, to whisper to us.

(For my part, we need never take the turn,
the route, could all day dawdle, stunned, assailed:
music and light, that year, seem route enough.
One might be quite happy never arriving.)

It is cold in the car, yet we keep warm
in ways not wholly understood, explained.
This is the one afternoon of the week
opera is coming to us from the Met.

Bidú Sayão, this very moment, listen,
the ocean not yet visible, the distance
splendid with prospects hinted at, translates
passion into Italian, lilting, melting,

joined by Mother, who, seated here beside me,
a collar of gray fox framing her face,
the four of us plunging south to the sea,
a mythic, fabled, possible Atlantic,

far from here a war raging, the gas rationed,
station by station shuttered, Broadway darkened,
breaks into the sweetest, purest Italian,
heart-stopping, poignant, lyrical, impassioned,

though we have never heard such language from her,
never known singing to such depth, nor guessed
what splendor she might harbor, what translucence,
though we have known her light in other contexts,

mimics Madame Sayão, spills with Puccini,
takes up that burden of romantic anguish
as though it were, in fact, hers to take up,
a sponsorship no less mysterious

to Mother, we suspect, than to my brother,
to Father, me, we who accompany her
in search of the Atlantic dumb, astonished,
more moved than, once, we thought we could be moved,

saying nothing, not knowing what to say,
or think, or do, at a loss what to feel,
the weight of all that issues from her awesome,
sumptuous, light-struck, opulent, Italian,

letting the opera spin out as it must,
letting music have its way, as it must,
or as one's life, later in the plot, must,
each element of chance, of choice, of risk,

what Rossini has envisioned as fate,
pursuing us who plunge south where the sea
glitters, refracts, repeats, over and over,
the name, the shape, the scope, of an arrival

not given us to know, not yet disclosed,
everywhere light assailing us, cascading,
in the car, past it, causeway, bay, surf, beach,
not least the mythic light of that Italian

raining down on Father, my brother, me,
the day cold, more than cold, but, in the back seat,
folded and tucked in lap robes as we are,
deep blue, sea-blue, nuzzled in fox, gray fox,

Madame Sayão and Mother in full voice,
in fullest voice, at the peak, so to speak,
of their careers, one mezzo-soprano
spurring the other on, ablaze, transcendent,

each, for the first time, soaring past her range,
past all ranges, in defiance of limits,
our maps arrayed before us on front seats
offering what Father might call "a view"

(though no map shall avail here, none, I tell you,
no front seat yield the vision, visions, promised,
and the thing Father may have had in mind
by "a view," whatever it may have been—

openings to the sky?, the sea?, a glimpse,
a half-glimpse, of horizons, destinations?—,
proves, once more, once more, to begin and end here,
here, in the car: one's self, one's self, not more)

one Saturday, or many, of that winter,
the first winter of the war, I am seven,
the day cold, more than cold, the Rockaways
as far, as problematic, as the sea,

that sea Father would have us hold a glimpse of,
if we are to hold anything, light pouring,
Broadway darkened, stations shuttered, gas rationed,
the Italian dense, rich, resplendent, flowing.

Certain Mysteries Flowing
from the Gown

"Miss Worth, as commanding a presence as ever in
an apricot Fortuny dress given to her by Lillian Gish,
cannot fail to hold her audience . . ." THE NEW YORK TIMES

for Stone Phillips

All that we know, all we shall need to know,
is that, tenderly folded, heaped in tissue,
laid in her hands, perhaps?, still in its box?,
the year obscured, the reason undisclosed,
before the fire at which they could have sat,
mythical fire, mythical light and warmth,

it was presented to Irene Worth—
a grace, a gift, an affluence, a wish
that you know splendor as, once, I, too, knew it—
by Miss Gish, who was launched on her career
perhaps a generation earlier
than Miss Worth, a career nurtured in silents

(now we proclaim it: subtleties, make entrance,
obsession take deep root, pursuit begin,
let history unfold here, ask the dream
to do what dream does best; let plot unravel
and explication implicate us all,
as, in the end, it shall, as it was meant to),

the designer Fortuny and the shade
not slate, not mauve, not lime, not anything

clearly unambiguous: apricot,
worn tonight by Miss Worth in her depiction
of what it is, or was, to be a woman
not playing Edith Wharton but a woman

reading to us the words of Edith Wharton,
letters, autobiography, those novels
of which it could be said they were forgotten,
relinquished by us, deemed unfashionable,
dated, genteel, yet clung to by a few,
a woman having Wharton tell us all,

nearly all, of what it was to be Wharton
precisely at the corner where the nineteenth
century happened unobtrusively,
without a cry, seemingly without effort,
into the twentieth, a lapse, a shift,
a turn so imperceptible, so seamless,

one could say of it that we barely noticed,
despite one's knowledge of that flaw in Wharton's
character—one of many, as she saw it—
which was to leave her with such meager talent,
none whatever, conspicuously lacking,
for turning matters singularly private

into subjects of public contemplation,
disclosures Edith Wharton never made,
could never make, confession foreign to her,
alien, as Henry James knew, to her nature—
there are places best left unlit, uncharted,
we can almost hear her say, though we know

she could never have brought herself to say it
(discretion: haunted by the thought of James
in need, under stress of financial burdens,

his novels in disfavor, selling poorly—
fashion had changed, or not yet caught up with him—,
she proposed that their publisher, Charles Scribner,

transfer her royalties to his account—
"advances against work our hope remains
we can expect in future," had they phrased it?—,
asking—no, not here, not in this—, *insisting*—
James was a proud man, sensitive, adroit
at distinguishing fact from fabrication,

at discerning "the figure in the carpet,"
however hidden, intricately patterned—
he not be told of the plot, never learn
of her hand in it, of that purity
of spirit, that nobility of gesture—
Wharton would be the last to call it that—,

informing all the woman thought and felt,
the delicacy of her step, her touch,
her concern centered solely on his comfort,
ease, on his freedom from distractions having
nothing to do with what the man was bent on,
all that, at last, at last, one knew to live for).

Whether Miss Gish, decades earlier, heard
Miss Worth, that April, in *The Cocktail Party*,
declaiming, eloquently, those long verse-lines
Eliot had composed to grace three acts—
mysteries of the human, of all things
to which we give permission to transform us

(could the poet have said, at the first run-through,
My dear Miss Worth, the play becomes redundant;
your voice, it seems, is poetry enough?);
whether, years later, Albee's *Tiny Alice*,

Miss Worth, that autumn evening, at her throat
a scarf the shade of lustrous apricots,

racing down Forty-first Street to the stage door—
seven minutes to curtain, places!, places!—,
Miss Gish, unrecognized, already seated,
sat in the dark of the tenth row, expectant,
hushed, waiting with the rest to be transformed,
are matters left, this late, to speculation.

(Had Edward Albee muttered to John Gielgud:
What must one feel, sharing a stage with her?;
enlarged, I should think, or perhaps diminished.)
Had Fortuny accepted a commission
Lillian Gish extended for a dress—
how had she put it?—utterly resplendent,

the shade astonishing, unprecedented,
standing that summer evening, as surmised,
at Mr. Griffith's massive, sculptured gates—
mythical cupids?, cherubs?, garlands?, bursts
of flowers to be seen in no known country?—,
feeling "quite pretty"—had she put it that way?—,

feeling, in her Fortuny, "quite transformed,"
one of the guests arriving at the party
to celebrate, at last, with Mr. Griffith
the final shot of *Orphans of the Storm*,
the filming over-budget, taxing, long.
Did Mr. Griffith sigh, bow, kiss her hand,

as courtly as before, yet newly stirred,
escort her to the ballroom, and beyond,
savor the splendor of a powdered shoulder,
understand, at last, what one might well live for?

Did ribbons, blue, grace Mary Pickford's hair?
Was Charlie Chaplin there, and did they dance?

Among the words which surfaced in his speech,
was Chaplin heard to utter, once, "resplendent,"
once whisper to Miss Gish she seemed "transformed"?
And was the weather kind, the evening fair?
I would ask, as well, of Monsieur Fortuny,
couturier extraordinaire, poor man,

his rôle, his gift, his flair, his feel for *luxe*,
the pride he may have felt, the sense of mission,
sleepless, returning to the workroom, late,
to view the thing once more, caress its folds,
telling Lillian Gish the shade she craved,
"unprecedented," "utterly resplendent,"

might be all but impossible to do—
"the only thing worth doing," her response?—:
pink is intractable, orange elusive;
apricot has one foot, Miss Gish, in each—
a mystery, a mix, a mystic footing—
but—our misfortune—both long to be elsewhere;

shall we try something simpler, then: beige?, teal?
And, equally, I seem to need to know
of seamstresses who lavished hope and care,
who came to feel love for it as they stitched,
the drapers and the fitters, twelve pale girls
employed to cut, to baste, to trim, to hem,

discreetly scatter glitter on the bodice,
a touch of soutache here, a sequin there,
the shirring raised, the gathers lowered, just so,
flow unto flow, a rising and a falling,

perfections of the life and of the art—
and at what cost?, one feels compelled to ask—,

so that Miss Gish know splendor in the evening,
know, once more, once more, what there was to live for,
astonishing through the first waltz, transcendent—
Chaplin enthralled, Griffith smitten, ecstatic—,
Irene Worth no less so, decades later,
reading one winter evening from Miss Wharton

(would that be how they phrased it, her "discretion,"
the grace in her which moved them most at Scribner's—
at what cost?—, left them shaken?), Henry James—
loving her motor cars, jaunts to be taken,
choices before one, roads, flow unto flow—
never far from the gleaming, transformed center.

Sophia and Marcello on a Bench

On a bench in the Bois, perhaps, a Paris
very much like Paris or not quite Paris,
yours to choose, a shade off, light not yet light
yielding the fabled contexts, vivid, just
(though the cinematographers go back,

go back again, mark lines, draw grids, plot angles,
mix, tinker, blend, not without qualms reshoot,
apprehensive, attempt to get it right,
attempt once more: so much devolves on *look*),
a cast less than the true cast, paler, dimmer,

making allowances for atmospherics,
a distant coast, another country, elsewhere,
that elsewhere plain speech breaks into pure song,
there, the true capital of gesture, nuance,
the streets, even the back streets, named for splendor,

where the filming took place, has yet to take place,
no matter, none, to us, to the director,
for whom, throughout, it is, it shall remain,
nothing less than unalterable, crucial,
that, at each turn, half-turn, we be transformed.

How to resolve what, from the start, one knows
to be utterly unresolvable:
in the Bois (early spring?, overcast?, April?),
this, it seems, is what they have come to do,
come one last time, their need, their task, their plight.

Difficulties abound, of course: you know that
merely viewing Marcello's face now, ravaged
by all one tried, but failed, to say, to do,
the weight of it incalculable, vast,
more intolerable than one imagines

on this side of a camera Robert Altman
strives to seduce us with from the beginning,
which, throughout, it will do, with our consent.
It was not this way thirty years ago:
Jeanne Moreau, in her anguish, stroked those features,

traveled like a blind woman with her fingers
over that face, knowing what she must do,
coaxed it back into life, what seemed like life,
though Michelangelo Antonioni
would never quite have put it that way, never

couch it in such terms nor be that specific
("Explain nothing; that shall have said it all").
Marcello's hair was dark that year, not white,
his features ravaged then, as well, but ravaged
with what their youth, his and Jeanne's, might transcend,

their glamour, that redeeming sense of presence
(overwhelming in those back-lighted scenes
played against walls, dense foliage, in which
Antonioni reaches for their anguish)
trivialized when spoken of as "style,"

might step across to light and turn their backs on,
the Borghese gardens themselves ripe, lush,
corners not threadbare, leaves not streaked with dust,
on the brink of pronouncements teeming, light-struck,
from which there was, could be, no turning back,

light into which, mid-distance, one could walk,
endlessly walk, sensing it was tomorrow,
the possible, oneself, to which one walked,
on the far edge, the limits of the frame
very nearly cropping it past our view,

a glimpse, no more, eyes half-closed, of a footpath
seeming to circle back upon itself
at the end of which some small conflagration
smolders where the last broken shards of light
shatter the wings of a stone angel placed there.

Altman, too, had attempted it, the year
his work went granular, dissolved in mist,
when all of it slid off to implication,
problematic, inundated, suspended,
borders dismantled overnight, abolished

(what would replace those maps made obsolete?),
disintegration trailing its subversions,
murkiness, the half-garbled, holding sway,
swept with the ambiguities he posed
and seemed, in fact, never to tire of posing—

concurrent dialogue, dense, overlapping,
players whose small arrivals and departures
each took place at the same time, in the same breath—
head turned, half-turned, glance, murmur, disappearance—,
through the same door, could he have brought himself

to seek enclosures here, demand nails, hammer,
two-by-fours, yield themselves to undertakings
as conclusive, as terminal, as doors,
a music wrought of coming and of going,
a choreography of dream and smoke,

Warren Beatty and Julie Christie turning
slowly—Altman draping them with a languor,
an indolence, so pronounced it would seem
barely a progress as they set off, early,
for a country, haze obscuring the borders,

never named but whose name you knew by heart
(explaining nothing will have told it all)—
into the raging of a thousand fractured
twilights, muted, mid-distance, each of which
had the look of tomorrow written on it,

snow glare, ice glitter, stands of pine and fir
impenetrable past where Altman took us,
would hope to take us, what awaited them
unutterable splendor in a Northwest
one part myth, the remainder Robert Altman,

that which astonishes, transcends, transforms,
lenses framing them lovingly, believing,
with the rest of us, daybreak, at the outset
of the journey, all things were possible,
given their youth, their restlessness, their passion,

their will to cross through anguish walking—where?,
set out on foot through snow pursuing—what?,
Altman just as succinct, explaining nothing,
refusing to name all that might have gripped them,
not drawing maps of difficult terrain,

having Warren turn to her, turn again,
turn as there seemed small need to turn before,
whisper, breath's vapor splintering the air,
beneath that clear, harsh light remove a glove,
the gesture private, touching, very nearly

ceremonial in its gravity,
its measuredness, raise a hand to her face,
a face, that year, as opulent as any,
graze Julie's neck and cheek with a bare palm
seen to tremble beneath what light assailed it,

in the distance, that house where Julie stayed,
clapboard saloon, beds-by-the-hour upstairs,
a small, smudged pane set in a smoke-framed window
glimpsing the pale, gilt wings of a tin angel
dangling from a thin wire above the bar.

II

The drama of the hat will draw us back
over and over, and to be drawn back
is to be drawn, each time, into oneself,
Sophia seated calmly, knees in place,
looking ahead, wearing sheer, black silk hose,

legs, quite moving, tucked sedately beneath her,
hands in her lap, Marcello (pleading?, begging?)
needing to speak, confide, confront, reveal,
searching for eloquence, poetry, even,
in a world not given to poetry,

finding within him speech, instead, mere speech,
plain speech, that speech given most men to speak,
all he can seem, this afternoon, to muster
under light one suspects falls without pity
in weather best called indeterminate

when it is not yet clear what else to call it,
defeat after defeat stamped on his face
like the map of the capital of failure

it comes, on these gray, French days, to resemble
(is there to be no end to transformation?).

(He and Jeanne sat in comparable light—
a choreography of dream and smoke?—,
light Antonioni called into being
for the occasion, south of here, the year
distant, half-glimpsed, if glimpsed at all, remembered

dimly all the while we were cultivating
our distractions, lived elsewhere, but remembered,
the year the public gardens seemed less public,
not exposed as they came to seem exposed—
exposure had not yet come into fashion

nor the belief all things could be explained—,
the dust not this intrusive, and the road
leading north to what one could only guess
had cypresses deployed to line its flanks
symmetrically, presences ghostly, still,

mysteriously self-possessed, a sign
rumors of order swept a universe
given triumphantly to the chaotic,
Jeanne and Marcello seated on a bench,
a stone bench, as recalled, Jeanne gloveless, hatless,

a flawless summer evening north of Rome,
her hair done simply—velvet clip, short bob—,
her dress black, shoes to match, only their breathing
separating them here, that narrow road
Antonioni favored film to film,

the possible, the still-to-be-explained,
receding, fading, presently, abandoned
to the dark the magician had arranged

to implicate them further, bring down on them,
in the name of all things that would transform.)

Sophia looks ahead, not to Marcello
(will she hear what the man has come to tell her?,
fasten on each word?, soften?, be persuaded?,
wear the mask of disdain she wore before?,
to the end cling to hope for transformation?),

despite this task on which he now seems bent,
the extremity of his desperation,
his struggle with the plainness of plain speech
he turns, half turns, to offer her, begins
(elsewhere it might be song; here, on this bench,

Paris, the Bois, leaves streaked with dust, all day
weather coming down, all day, call it speech:
what else might carry on such paltry air?),
her hands folded demurely in her lap
across the small, flat purse—a clutch?—whose shade

matches the cape she lets fall from her shoulders
so brilliantly, to such languorous purpose,
one is convinced beneath each move she makes,
each turn she takes, each step, each breath, or fails to,
lies opulence beyond premeditation,

a richness of intent well past intent,
the folds of the cape, gathered fold on fold,
sweeping to calf, to mid-calf, flowing past it,
spilling nearly to the grass where their feet rest—
an ordinary cape, but in her hands,

her touch casual, delicate, seductive,
the fabric of momentous embarkation,
its shade matching the vast, billowing hat

whose task it is to reveal, to conceal,
both at once, turn, half-turn, entering, leaving

(is there to be no end to what transforms us?),
this hat whose circularity portends
no beginning, no end, sumptuous sail
(silk?, linen?, felt?, velour?) part dream, part smoke,
part anything one might have wished it to be,

beneath whose crown Sophia all day sits,
peers, ponders, poses, sits, momentous hat
whose gift it is, shall be, to draw us back
into the swoops, the contexts, of its myth,
this dreamscape in the midst of which she waits,

unfathomable, shimmering, discrete,
the dreamt of, longed for, held to, which insists
there be no end, no end, to transformation.
(Was the weather the weather Altman wished?;
was Paris Paris as the mind's eye glimpsed it?

Are we to be drawn back not by the hat
but by the dream and smoke in which two others,
another park, a distant light, the year
unrecognizable, a narrow road
seen narrowing, once sat, bereft, enveloped?)

Say, if you can, what held us, holds, transforms,
what Marcello—banished that day?, embraced?—
was overheard, that afternoon, to plead,
whether Sophia faced him, touched him, wept,
Antonioni, distant park, wrenched light,

an elsewhere speech may well break into song,
panning north to that road—the journey taxing,

the crossing dust-streaked—where there is positioned
(the art director's touch or the magician's?)
a bleak angel, irredeemably stricken,

barely glimpsed at the same time glimpsed too clearly,
standing clenched and forlorn in a small park
not quite a park, by the side of that road
not yet a road, reputed to lead north
where north, true north, shall wholly fail to lie,

the route into the capital of failure,
rumor has it—, standing desolate, drenched,
snaring fragments of darkness coming down
in the folds, fold on fold—no end, no end—
of the devastation lighting its wings.

III

She was photographed at the Paris Opéra
one year, her sons flanking her in a box,
crowns for embellishment, swatches of velvet,
by tradition reserved for royalty,
front, extreme right, fringed tassels, plaster cherubs,

gold leaf on gold leaf, overlay of grape leaves,
both boys rising as if on cue to bow
when introduced during the intermission—
Act Two of *Carmen*, Solti the conductor—,
two splendid youths, dark-haired Italian princes,

luminous in black dinner jackets, white ties,
on leave at Easter from Swiss boarding schools—
skiing at Val d'Isère?, sailing off Hydra?—,
graceful rising from carved, brocaded chairs,
reserved, respectful, wholly self-contained,

their gestures measured, their bows courtly, spare,
striding effortlessly, one could foretell,
into the pure flame of a thousand fractured
twilights splintering glitter on horizons
raging from here to unnamed parts and back,

if need be—naming nothing names it all—,
a choreography of dream and smoke,
a distant coast, another country, elsewhere,
that elsewhere speech is breaking into song,
that narrow road Antonioni panned to

tirelessly, seeming never to weary
of the glimpse, of the view, never to turn from
certain perplexing vaguenesses—light?, half-light?,
angle of vision?, lens?, the view itself?—,
presences manifest film after film,

holding the endless promise of fresh starts,
beginnings, embarkations, a terrain—
cypresses, road-not-road, horizon, wings—
brimming with premonition, implication,
where, even now, now, this late, lost, obscured,

however parched the ground on which one stood,
hoped to stand, failed to, footing awkward, missed,
one's life, even now, there, past the viewfinder,
there, the true capital of gesture, nuance,
might lie, might wait, there, to set out for, suffer.

What was her life? Had Carlo Ponti loved her?
What year had she acquired a taste for *Carmen*?,
for opera?, velvet?, for the royal box?,
boeuf-en-croûte, haute couture, a blanc de blanc
she would deem not too sweet yet not too "sec,"

one or two sips, no more, thin, crystal goblet,
the wine steward, hovering, apprehensive,
not yet guessing what the verdict might be,
whether yes would come from her, whether no?
Had Ponti taught which fork to use for salad?

How had she gone about fashioning sons
who, when the time was right, would know to rise,
rise slowly, gravely, patiently, from chairs
splendidly carved, intricately brocaded,
choreography of dream and smoke,

all things at once, or none, private, enclosed,
to rise, to bow, to wear with such resplendence
the evening clothes they wore, supremely wore—
beyond the Opéra Paris, April, starlit,
breaking into unutterable splendor,

song, even, should song have been called for, summoned—,
to face, when asked, the audience they faced
(no end to bows, turns not quite turns, to facing),
the musicians having put down Bizet,
baton at rest, bows, pedals, levers, keys,

introduction made, recognition given,
their gaze so modest, clear-eyed, indrawn, spare,
an utter self-possession under lights
dimmed that Solti might briefly leave the pit,
might renew himself for the final act?

Who was it taught the hoisting of the sails
on a course south-southeast, Hydra to Corfu,
their arms thrust high above their heads, the jib
gripped fiercely in both hands, tacking to starboard,
canvas whipping above them, salt-streaked, lashed?

Or, Val d'Isère ablaze with light, dense light,
swaying beneath them down the slope—look at it,
look at it, boys, flame, pure flame, look—, the knack
of persuading the wrists to splay the poles
flush with the ice they clung to, should the run

seem to offer resistance, elevation
extended, speed intensified, the glitter
into which we are faced prolonged, the trick—
difficult, fraught with risk, yet wholly crucial—
of looking too intently at the sun

yet, for all that, somehow eluding blindness?,
spared none of it, none of it, yet demanding
to see, see more, again, no end to seeing,
no end to salt—who taught them?—, wave on wave.
Is there to be no end to what transforms us?

Was she who she had been that year in outskirts
clinging to Naples (could she say Pozzuoli
and not choke on those syllables, not cry out
Someone else, someone else, not I, I tell you,
not who I am, not the one I became?),

pale girl with skirts patched from pillow slips, dust rags,
begging the Americans for stale bread,
a bowl of rice from the field mess, hard candy,
scrambling for apples they would toss from tanks
they sat astride, cowboys mounted on horses,

Sophia of the scraped knees and torn elbows,
Sophia, having made her way from Pozzuoli—
luminous, twilit evening, spring, mid-April,
the first stars, mythic, rising on a Paris
very much like Paris or not quite Paris—

to the enchantments of the royal box,
that elsewhere speech breaks into pure, sweet song,
gold leaf on gold leaf, cherubs, tassels, velvet,
having entered discreetly, somewhat breathless
(late?, the journey taxing?, the crossing dust-streaked?:

is there to be no end, then, none whatever?),
waiting for Solti, house lights dimmed, Bizet,
in the Bois Paris breaking into splendor,
the third act, resolution, transformation,
to the right, to the left, holding the flanks,

stand-ins for princes at the Court of Venice
(who had taught them which fork to use for salad?),
two dark-haired youths rising from slender chairs
magnificently carved, richly brocaded,
sons rising as sons never rose before

(arms above heads, hoisting Aegean sails?;
wrists lashed to poles, tracking the downhill slope?),
Sophia looking, looking to them, light-struck
(look at the sun, look at it, look, boys, risk it),
Sophia, ragged elbows, Dior hats—

someone else, someone else, another life—
whose gift it is, shall be, to draw us back,
and back, know no end to the drawing back,
on the rim of her gown, chiffon, contingent
on how she moves, on house lights, Solti's entrance,

a small clip, diamonds, breaking into flame
(ice at Val d'Isère?, surf thrashing off Hydra?)
searing the wings—had Ponti loved her, shaped her?—,
delicate, tipped with emeralds—look, boys, risk it—,
of the angel pinned to the velvet bodice.

Ultimate Poem

One takes the dark valise that one has taken
on specific occasions before this
when there were voyages to be embarked on.

What recommends it is, simply, its size:
small enough to hold just what it should hold,
just what one wishes, or needs, it to hold.

The morning of departure, but not sooner
(readiness plays no part: one can be said
to be as ready to leave as not ready),

one places in it (fever slowly mounting
as one handles each object) the essentials:
soap, a small towel, pencils, paper, swim trunks.

One's hopes run high. Flushed with anticipation
of distance, distances, drunk with the prospect
of whatever may still be possible

in one's life, south of here, the fierce, bleached splendor
of exploration, sensing how light pours there,
how the surf breaks there, how the dark comes down,

one is nevertheless visibly cautious
not to betray, too much, too soon, too deeply,
the precise nature (word, or glance, or gesture)

of what it is to be possessed by that,
gripped by the sum of the still-undisclosed.
(What is the word with which one translates fever?)

Nor need that coast be named yet in this poem,
though it may be enough, more than enough,
to know its syllables lie drenched with music,

music more intimate, perhaps, or darker,
more moving, left to one's imagination.
One travels south, far south. There is a beach

(rather, mile upon mile of dazzling beaches),
a long strand sweeping out from where one stands,
from wherever one stands, in all directions.

One arrives, of course, without reservations
at a hotel neither crumbling nor grand.
It may be better not to be expected

nor, when asked, to give one's name at the desk,
never to say where one has been before this
nor to reveal where one may venture next.

Be vague, elusive, abstract, noncommittal:
I may just stay, you say, indefinitely,
or: I have not decided what my plans are.

A boy who may be named Fernando shows you
your room, takes your valise (You travel light),
opens the terrace door, waits for your tip.

You thank him. When he leaves, you look about you.
Not finding what you want, you call the desk:
Could you provide a table, nothing large,

I might keep on the balcony to write on?
And could these curtains (sheer, white muslin curtains,
if there are curtains) be stripped from the windows?

I want to have whatever light comes down,
whatever darkness, for that matter, too.
A boy who may be named Emilio enters

at six, bearing a table on his back,
a small, square, wooden table, its four legs
listing to starboard when he sets it down.

You want to write on this? he asks. I nod
I thought I'd write while looking out to sea.
He moves the table to the balcony.

Like this?, he asks. Like that, I say, and thank him.
You want the curtains down?, he asks. Yes, please.
He makes the tour, one window, then the next,

standing on a chair carefully removes
one sheer, white muslin curtain, then another,
if there are curtains, holds them to the light,

where they dangle and sway from his bare arm.
You don't like curtains?, he asks. I want light,
more light; I want as much as I can have.

(This is enough for a boy sent upstairs
on a mission having to do with curtains,
with lights, more light, with small, crude, wooden tables,

enough for a boy who may, or may not,
be named Diego. One nods, smiles, says Thank you,
explaining nothing, all the while, nothing, nothing.)

I place a book beneath one buckled leg,
a cigarette pack, ancient, musty, found
in the bureau drawer, beneath another.

I rock it back and forth. It hardly moves now.
I undress, store my clothes. Light pours, light pours.
I change into the swim trunks I have brought.

Arrayed in scales of green-gold, iridescent,
a baby lizard strolls across one wall
for a glimpse of Room 201's new guest,

closing and opening its armored lids
with some momentous effort (one should look
wisely, judiciously, or not at all).

From the valise, propped high on the low bed,
I take the pencils first, immensely yellow,
lacquered finishes blazing in the sun,

in ascending order, shortest to tallest,
according to length line them on the table,
their points flawless, immaculate, black, gleaming.

Then I remove the paper I have brought,
blindingly white, crisp, unlined, neither weighted
nor flimsy, unbound sheets which seem almost

eager to rise to take whatever mark
one might be called upon to draw across them
(the word for light, perhaps, the word for evening).

I sit now at the table, feel the heat
settle like birds, great birds, on both my shoulders,
one on each, see a swimmer take the breakers

as opulently as the sea takes light.
Soon the dark will have changed the sky to water,
or the water to sky, it hardly matters.

Wild bougainvillea rattles the bright shutters.
One's eye travels to the first of the pencils.
I touch it, grip it tenderly, begin.

This is the poem one has come to write,
the poem one thinks of as ultimate.
This is the music, this, one had in mind.

Now the Fitzgerald Brothers
Growing Older

for Lynne Sharon Schwartz

It was, it seemed, what everyone did that year,
or hoped to do, they no less than the others,
that brief, first year, after returning: married,
both just home from the war, virile young men,
measured, reserved, yet not ungainly with it,
men with quiet voices and quiet eyes,
a certain wayward grace to how they moved,
using their share of words cautiously, sparely,
as though believing few would be affected
by what they thought, or felt, by what they said,
persuaded, too, there may be certain limits
to the words one might spend, things one might say,
limits, in fact, to what language could do,
could not do, in a world seemingly given
neither to speech nor feeling but to fact,
the plain fact, or the bare fact, but the fact,
to things incontrovertible, foreclosed,
subject no longer to interpretation.
One's knowledge of it, of that year, of them,
even, possibly, of oneself, one's insight
into those complications past one's view,
subtleties, half-tones, shadings, is quite sketchy:
how can one hope to read the lives of others,
even—perhaps more difficult—one's own?;
yet, once more, we attempt it, we persist,
relentlessly, not easily dissuaded
from the effort, the hope of understanding
what, in the end, eludes all understanding.

Home from the war, reticent, young, attractive,
each married—the first girls they met, it seemed,
or the first ones, when asked, who answered yes
(all of it soon, too soon, the choice too hurried,
David and Lyle methodical, slow, cautious,
in all things before this—but who can know?
And what of need, how to account for need,
fail to account, in the lives others live,
in the choices others make, fail to make?),
the girls themselves, should they have been prevailed on,
able, no doubt, to offer their own versions,
further views of the context from perspectives
not quite envisioned before this, now lost,
gathered into the rhythms of the telling—,
so it appeared that year, though I forget much,
need, perhaps, to forget much: Lyle to someone
long-legged, small-waisted, hair straight, drab mud-brown,
silent, awkward with those she did not know
(and there were few she knew), bringing with her
a daughter ten months old from her first marriage,
balancing her in one arm on the front steps
the day she was to move in (standing there
hesitant, still, not knowing what to do
nor how to do it, if it should be done—
mount the stairs?, breathe?, not breathe?, move?, cease from movement?,
stand as still as one has ever stood still?,
not yet told Please come in nor Leave at once,
as though it were her house yet someone else's,
something of both, perhaps, something of neither,
and where she stood, between, the footing shaky,
Lyle's bride, yet an intruder), with the other
struggling to manage two battered valises,
desolate-looking, haunted, black, forlorn,
jammed with the remains of a life before this,
buttons, hand mirror, twine, yellowing postcards

(views of Paris?, of Louisville, Kentucky?)
streaked with coffee stains, undecipherable,
hairbrush, needles, a stack of photographs
bound, late one evening, with two rubber bands,
in disarray, no doubt the last thing snatched
before she had been able to escape—
the only word—, perhaps in time, perhaps not;
David to a girl later to be called,
called by David himself, in fact, "my floozy,"
a girl from Cincinnati, pudgy, giggler,
incessant giggler, tier on dazzling tier
of freshly coiffed, cascading golden ringlets,
a shade, she boasted, listed as Champagne
on the color charts hung in each small shoppe,
each little back-room salon, dedicated
ultimately to one idea, one
(and no matter how tenuous, how frail,
how arbitrary, temporary, brief,
the myth, the vision, the ambition): beauty,
the possibility of blonde perfection,
spreading like contagion through the hill towns
of the green reaches of southern Ohio.
Nothing much went right for them after that,
though it is to the couples I refer,
not the brothers, who, for reasons not known then,
were to lead wholly another existence,
individual, separate, private, spared.

They bought adjoining houses, fenced yards, gables,
what they thought they would need, would grow to need,
attics fashioned into what were called "studies,"
"sitting rooms" on the main floor where, each claimed,
visitors, through the years, would be received,
guests destined, as it happened, time passed, passing,
neither to be invited nor received.
Saturdays were given to cutting lawns,

trimming the hedges, most particularly
the hedge, the common hedge, between them, shared,
that with special attention to detail,
embellished, re-embellished, shaped, reshaped,
a gift for architectural refinement,
proportion, balance, symmetry, perspective,
neither suspected in himself before.
Each had retrievers, pure gold, walked them, evenings,
twilight half-obscuring the path they took,
together to the nearby lake and back
where the first stars rose, then the moon, where darkness
found their faces, placed its burden across
their shoulders (if not yet, that year, their lives)
with a gentleness wholly unexpected.
The brides, beside each other in the rows,
stooped over seedlings, bulbs, hands sore, nicked, grimy,
planted, as each was given to plant, tulips,
although, still giggling, freshly coiffed, My Floozy
was heard to tell the neighbors, those who listened,
tulips were not, could never be, her "style,"
yard work was not what she was born to do,
she, a girl renowned down the Interstate
for hair destined, in time, to be described
through the vast and anonymous green reaches
of what they attempt to identify,
still, improbably, as southern Ohio,
with one word, one, stunning, succinct: Champagne.
Five months after she came (longer for her
than for David and Lyle, who had, together,
one or two days returned, that year, from war,
no ceremony marking the occasion,
a private moment, known to just the two,
buried their watches in warped bottom drawers
of antique bureaus stored in upstairs studies
each carved from space in cramped third-story attics,
never bothered with clocks, with time, again,

one more distraction eagerly dispensed with),
five months languishing, blondeness wrought for naught,
champagne perfections lost, quite lost, on all,
she left the house one morning, giggling stopped,
perfumed, high-heeled, rouged, ringlets each in place,
bearing a list, a short list—"rye, dark," "butter,"
"peaches, only if ripe"—, and sixty dollars,
the note for David reading BACK IN MINUTES.
Leaving behind the yard work, roots no weeding,
no degree of persistence, could set right,
hibiscus, lavender, no tenderness,
no heart brimming with patience, get to grow straight,
the delicately stippled but failed tulips,
symbol of all her time there was, was not,
Champagne, on the first bus to the sublime,
Champagne, striving for beauty, an idea
of perfection, the possible, the rare,
quite far from David and quite far from Lyle,
each, together, was never seen again.

It was two or three mornings later David
noticed that she was gone, perhaps at breakfast,
a slice of toast, quite dry, fried egg, black coffee,
reaching for bread, rye-dark, which was not there.

They walk the dogs at evening, the retrievers,
new pups this year, as golden as before,
even more lustrous than the ones recalled
(it seems a strange tale; one needs to forget
perhaps as much, or more, as one remembers,
make allowances for the variations
in tone, in shape, in texture, time inflicts,
time or the need to muffle the tale's impact,
soften the coloration, blur details),
watch the stars, night to night, in their ascension,
glimpse the moon, through all seasons, in its phases,

lighting the half-dark surface of the lake,
take the path they have taken in the evening
through twenty years of evenings, there and back,
still half-obscured by darkness falling, fallen,
by whatever is destined yet to fall.
Saturdays are still given to the lawns
(one wished to say, but did not say, "devoted");
by spring one knows the hedges will be shorn,
most notably the one they share, between them,
the hedge they work together, slowly, slowly,
riveting, touching patience, flawless care,
shaping, working, reworking, once more shaping,
each from his side, each working deftly inward,
trimmed—and one's task will be to do it justice—
much like their lives, it seems now, of all excess,
pruned of error, distraction, undue grossness,
each working from his side, miscalculation.

Lyle's wife is still there, little seen, less heard
(her name escapes me now, as it did then;
is it possible it was never spoken
in the years, twenty years, since she arrived?,
standing one morning on the doorstep, baby
in her arm, awkward, thin, angular, gawky,
stranger in this man's house—in all men's houses?—,
waiting for Yes, for No, for Welcome, Enter,
the wait, time passed, time passing, unavailing,
the life lived, not lived, equal to the wait.
"Lyle's wife" is all I knew, is all I know,
which seemed enough, more than enough, still seems so),
by April making scratch marks in dry earth,
finding a cause in yard work, banking tulips
with what sustenance they still need to bloom,
raging quietly in the small, neat bed
Lyle fashioned from wood chips, stone, terra cotta—
after twenty years in her care, the same bulbs

breaking into pure splendor, twenty years!—,
making the same short lists David's wife made
while staring, mornings, at the kitchen floor
("rye, dark," "butter," "peaches, only if ripe"),
except that each time Lyle's wife leaves the house,
closes the door behind her (faintly shudders?),
she knows, knows well, the way back, seems resigned
(what can one know of others' lives?) to take it,
opens the gate, returning, climbs those steps
where she stood waiting, twenty years before,
washes the breakfast dishes, scrubs the floor.
It is years since her daughter left; a postcard
(addressed simply to "Lyle's wife," nothing more)
may, or may not, at intervals, arrive,
time difficult, at best, to place, to measure
(views of Paris?, of Louisville, Kentucky?,
the distance equal, the name not important),
the only thing that matters, nameless, faceless,
unable to be rendered ("Hope all's well,
I'm fine. Best to you, C"), lost, wholly lost.

(That year, when Lyle returned and bought the house,
began to shape the common hedge with David,
each working slowly inward from his side,
scrupulous, loving care, crucial attention—
it was a month or two before they married,
before they both went out in search of brides,
what it was time to do, they thought, and did—,
I spent days in the window seat, note paper
scattered across the carpet, practicing
the signature of who I would become,
perfecting, scroll by scroll, elaboration
after elaboration, "Anne Fitzgerald,"
Anne, Lyle's wife, Lyle's bride, seventeen that summer,
"Anne Fitzgerald," and again: "Anne Fitzgerald,"
loving the way it looked, fit, seemed to fit,

expected it would come, come soon, to fit.
But it was long ago, too long ago;
I forget much, need to forget much, *need* to.)

Lyle's beard is shading softly into gray now,
subtly, quite delicately, nothing shocking,
nothing overnight, nothing hard to live with,
just as one would expect Lyle's beard to shade,
would expect Lyle's life slowly to unfold.
Uncannily, the beard that David grew
the very year that Lyle's was coming in
has gone gray in the same way, just as subtly,
light against dark, dark playing off the light,
margins stippled, the center black, pure black.
Lyle seems just as impressive, time passed, passing,
the older he becomes, possibly more so;
a deeper stillness in him, something prouder
in the bearing, the carriage, greater richness
in the light flowing upward from the bones —
the certainty of who he has become? —,
something immeasurable, fiercer, darker
(how is one to read intimate, small gestures,
passion in the life of another, longing?).

I see them in the evening, late, past midnight,
the weather of no consequence whatever
(can they be said even to notice weather?,
as though nothing could harm them now, befall them,
nothing for which they would not be prepared,
nothing they might not come back whole from, spared),
setting off on their bicycles together
for the long night ride into — into what?,
the border of the county drawn quite clearly,
invisible yet marked, just past the woods,
or the county beyond, who can be certain,
lacking a proper map, without the feel

of the terrain beneath one's feet, the wind
slamming one's face, the dark lashing one's back?;
or climbing to the roof to nurse the hoot owl
which, unaccountably, chooses to roost there
midway along the slate roof which divides them
(I wished to say "unites" but kept from saying),
the common roof they share, the passageway
of which, viewed from below, one cannot say
this is David's, legally, this is Lyle's,
as the document specifies, the deed
drawn at the county courthouse in their names,
David begins here, just here, Lyle ends there,
even the owl's confusion, it would seem,
its refusal to choose, to mark the border,
to say precisely where it is it stands,
or nests, or roosts, or ekes out its owl life
these clear, resplendent evenings of late summer,
or, omen it becomes now, haunts the dreams,
time passed, time passing, both Fitzgeralds dream,
the common dream, the shared dream, Lyle and David,
returning from the long ride into—what?,
perspiring, cheeks flushed, muscles taut, hearts pounding,
exhausted and exhilarated both,
each working, slowly, inward from his side,
unseen but seen by the other on his,
of the shared hedge, the shared roof, the shared life,
working inexorably, twenty years,
trimming error, miscalculation, excess,
pruning the dross of foolishness, distraction,
to the only position possible,
passion sustained, sustaining, in a world
given neither to single-mindedness
nor the ecstasies, sorrows, of obsession:
the heart, the very heart, true, truest, center.

Jack Waiting

in memory, JFK

All that we know, all we may need to know,
is that glimpse of him, turning, looking back,
not the looking back but the turn to look back
(what is it, early, he would hope to see,
peering and peering, but not yet quite see?),

the quintessential gesture of a youth
standing there on the verge of—moments after
the picture would be taken—embarkation,
tracking south on the morning, dense fog lifting,
light soon to break here, soon the day on fire.

There is this picture of him—midway through
the haunted Thirties?, from the dimness looming,
shall one guess it may be six in the morning?,
weather indeterminate?, the terrain
familiar yet unlikely?—on the beach,

wakened moments ago, waiting to sail,
though no prows are yet visible, no sails,
and the sea must remain conjecture, rumor,
standing alone, yes, but, more accurately,
standing utterly clear-eyed, self-possessed,

wearing rumpled, gray sweatshirt, battered sneakers,
a look at once both innocent and knowing
(do our looks soon become us, we our looks?),
and those trousers of which it might be said
these are trousers which have seen better days,

although one senses there could not be days
better than these, days of one's nineteenth summer,
the salt of embarkation on the wind,
a tacking south, a prow, bleached canvas, landfall,
half turning to look back at the viewfinder

whose task it is, it was, to find the view
that grips us, holds us, tells us, gives us names,
if not dispel the ambiguity
which, with the mist, clings to us here this morning,
manage, fittingly, somehow to compound it.

Once it was this way, once the August sun
had yet to rise, daylight had yet to break,
one's life had yet to open, as it would,
into one hundred unimaginable
fragments, distances, myths, amazements, more,

each with its intricacies, splendor, heat,
of which it has been given to us to know
nothing, this morning, mist obscuring all,
on a beach in the dream called Massachusetts,
the subject, hair uncombed, waiting for light.

Once it was possible to turn this way,
half turn, look back, yet still not quite look back
(one is early, nineteen: the Thirties shroud us);
all that, later, one might well have looked back on
has yet to take place, youth is raw youth, no more,

and whatever is bound to break, break here,
break beyond anything to be imagined,
is not even a wisp on the horizon;
where soon, as one surmises, sails appear,
prows, whipping canvas, oh, the fabled landfalls,

nothing as yet appears, and where the crews,
sweatshirts, sneakers, trousers from better days,
are rumored to assemble on the beach
in the dream of the dream called Massachusetts,
no banter is exchanged, no laughter heard.

On the reverse of the photograph someone,
perhaps a week after the shot was taken,
needing to place it past forgetting, loss,
has drawn, indelibly, eleven letters
on the smooth backing, letters slanting right,

precipitous the angle of ascent,
the printing neat, exact, upper left corner,
the space between each letter measured, even,
the strokes careful, patient, artfully done,
the caption reading, dark blue ink, JACK WAITING,

nothing separating the two words—hyphen,
comma, dash, colon—, that alone: JACK WAITING
(once it was this way, once, nineteen, mist rising,
August, on the beach, early, once: remember),
a bleach mark (grain of salt?, drop of sea water?,

random smudge a forefinger left on paper
as a hand held the pen to shape the letters?),
pale now, its intensity dissipated,
whirled at the center, lace fringing the edges,
stopping just short of the letters themselves,

the devastation seemingly contained
within the borders of a mere half-inch—
map of a foreign country never named—,
the two words spared, intact, blue ink still vivid,
as precipitous as before: JACK WAITING—

time?, weather?, the damages at work here,
by whatever names they present themselves
(once, August, early, on the beach: remember)
and in whatever guise they choose to enter
(sweatshirt, sneakers, hair uncombed, fabled trousers)?

However difficult the task may prove
(the place from which to view it, where to stand,
where, past forgetting, not to stand, position
of picture-taker in regard to subject—
not the looking back but the turn to look back—;

matters of intervention, distance, light,
availing light, the light that makes the dark
even more wrenching, infamous, pervasive;
judgments reached as to what is best left out—
subtleties made more telling by their absence—;

aspects of a discretionary nature
too problematic to broach fully here—
to crop, to frame, to edit, do without:
what can be sacrificed, what can be saved;
the anguish of photography itself),

what I would have, as well, would be a picture—
unposed, unplanned, beyond the reach of art,
past all considerations of "arrangement"—
of weather bearing witness in a life,
thine own collaborator, hushed accomplice

(I have this picture of him, nineteen, turning,
light soon to break here, soon the day on fire,
early, early enough in Massachusetts
that devastation seems, for now, contained),
done wholly in those tones, half-tones, of loss,

unremitting, which alone do it justice,
done so that one would be hard-pressed to tell
where JACK WAITING begins, where weather ends,
the distances between to no avail,
minor distinctions relevant no longer

(no slowly waking crews as yet assemble,
no salt-bleached canvas blinds us, mythic prows
have yet to haul their dreamscapes into view;
is devastation seemingly sequential?,
the damages at work here bordered, named?),

the quintessential gesture—turn, half-turn,
the turning to look back, not the look back—
of a youth facing into the viewfinder
on the beach in the dream called Massachusetts
(uncombed conspirator, thine own accomplice),

unwittingly determining himself—
is this what one is fated, then, to do?—
what shall be sacrificed, what shall be saved,
fragments, distances, myths, amazements, more,
not yet made, soon made (once, remember, once),

enough, more than enough, to have us know,
early, or late, the youth in question clear-eyed
(the anguish of photography), caught waiting,
the thing that comes, at last, to break the heart
breaks it interminably, as suspected.